Contemporary Piano Method
book 2B

by Margaret Brandman

Exclusive distributors for Australia and New Zealand
Encore Music Distributors
227 Napier St, Fitzroy VIC 3065 Australia
Phone +61 3 9415 6677
Facsimile +61 3 9415 6655
Email sales@encoremusic.com.au

This book © Copyright 2015 by Margaret Brandman trading as Jazzem Music
46 Gerrale St, Cronulla NSW 2230 Australia
ISBN 978-0-949683-26-7
ORDER NUMBER MMP 8025
International copyright secured (APRA/AMCOS). All rights reserved.

Unauthorised reproduction of any part of this publication by any means,
including photocopying, is an infringement of copyright.

CONTEMPORARY PIANO METHOD - BOOK 2B

INTRODUCTION

This method is designed to equip the student with the necessary skills to play both Classical and Modern music, including Popular and Jazz styles, with ease and understanding while giving experience in skills required for both classical and contemporary examination syllabi. The piano method is the central core of an integrated course which provides materials for ear-training (audio and workbooks), theory, technique, improvisation and repertoire pieces in all styles.

The methodology incorporates various learning styles or modalities, including:

* aural training
* spatial reasoning -visual, aural and tactile
* colour - to impart the meanings of the durations of the notes
* visualisation and the use of pictorial representations of the intervals
* the gestalt approach to topics (the whole view)
* knowledge of keyboard geography
* shape and pattern reading
* harmonic analysis
* improvisation
* transposition

Following on from book 2A in the series, this next book continues to feature:

The streamlined interval approach to reading
This is achieved when the aural, tactile and visual aspects of music are combined so that students are able to read and play by following the flow of intervals. Level Two develops the *music speed-reading and learning skills* to a high degree. by encouraging performers to view sections as larger recognisable musical shapes and patterns, including those which span an octave.

Transposition
By combining the interval reading approach with *scale pattern thinking*, students are able to transpose music to other keys with ease. The added benefit of this skill is the security that is instilled in the performer for reading music in the written position in the more advanced keys.

Easy ways to conceptualise rhythm and rhythm notation
The use of diagrams to be coloured in and clapped helps students to quickly associate a concrete meaning to the language of music rhythm notation and to establish a body feel for timing. The use of colour, spatial concepts and the tactile information transferred by the act of colouring, brings into play many accelerated learning concepts.

Keyboard Geography
The *keyboard pattern approach* is used to teach both all major and all minor scales in all forms. Students are required to close eyes and visualise their hands on the keyboard pattern for the key, before playing the scale and reading the music. Refer to the pictorial patterns for Major scales on page 102 of Book 2A and to the supporting publication *Pictorial Patterns for Keyboard Scales* and Chords for all the *minor* patterns.

Understanding Harmonic Structure and Modulation
A unique feature of this course is that it requires students to be actively engaged in the task of discovering the underlying harmonic structure of music, using the information to speed up the learning process, build an aural awareness of keys and chords, and to use as a basis for improvisation.

Adding to the knowledge of all the scale tone triads in major and minor keys and the dominant and diminished 7th chords gained in Book 2A, this next book, introduces some of the common chromatic chords, and the other standard sixth and seventh chords.

Meanwhile, the harmonic palette is further to include modulation to related keys. See pages 200 and 201 for the Contemporary Piano Method's unique template to be completed for modulation to the six closely related keys for music of the baroque and classical period. (It looks rather like an unusual insect with six legs - and is therefore called a Modulation Spider!) . This template can be photocopied and used to discover the modulations and family of chords for each new key.

Improvisation
The knowledge of the sounds of scales and chords and the keyboard patterns for them is fostered so that they can be used as tools for improvisation. In this book the I vi ii V I progressions are extended to encompass progressions based on the entire Cycle of Fifths. This progression will be used in songs and as a vehicle for improvisation.

Styles of Music
This book features contemporary dance rhythms including rock, latin-american and jazz, giving the styles and experience required to become both a professional musician in the popular field, and a competent and informed performer of classical music. Parallels are drawn between the harmonic devices of the classical and modern composers.

Books 3 and 4 of this series build upon the information in this book and move on to cover more advanced Classical, Jazz and Contemporary techniques and the harmonic understanding required for those levels. Topics include: unusual scales, extended and altered chords, modern writing techniques, reading in C Clef, Figured Harmony at the keyboard, Polyphony and many other related topics.

For more detailed information on the ideas and information in the series refer to my web site:

www.margaretbrandman.com

Margaret Brandman (Dr)
Ph.D (Mus/Arts), B.Mus.(Comp), T.Mus.A
F.Comp. ASMC., F.Mus.Ed.ASMC., L.Perf. ASMC
Hon.FNMSM., A.Mus.A., ASA T.Dip

See page 203 for a list of integrated support materials including theory and aural to use with this method.

CONTEMPORARY PIANO METHOD
BOOK TWO
CONTENTS   PART   A

Musical Styles Through the Ages	8
Reading Music	9
Interval Review	10
Review Exercises	11
Counting and Colouring Review	12
Major Scale Review. Cycle of Fifths	14
No. 1 A Little Joke, Brandman. (Mezzo Staccato)	15
Tetrads (Four-Note Chords)	16
No. 2 Russian Folk Song, Beethoven. Primary Triad Review	17
Minor Scales **A Minor**	18
Handy Manuscript Page	20
E Minor Scale New Position Changing Methods Number One Interval Climbers (Fifths)	21
Minor Chords **A and E Minor**	22
No. 3 Winter Waltz, Brandman. How to find the Key	23
Minor Chords in the Major Scale and Major Chord Table. **Phrasing**	24
No. 4 Serenade, Haydn	25
Passing and Auxiliary Notes Music Speed Reading: Interval Climbers (Sixths)	26
No. 5 Jerry's Jump, Brandman (D.C. al Fine)	27
B, D and G Minor Scales and Chords	28
Music Speed Reading: Sixth and Seventh Chord Shapes	30
No. 6 Signs of the Times, Brandman (Dal Segno and Coda)	31
No. 7 Scaling Mount Neverest, Brandman (8va and Loco)	32-33
Naming Intervals	34
Music Speed Reading: Interval Climbers (Sevenths). Accents	36
No. 8 Spanish Accent, Brandman	37
Diminished and Augmented Chords	38
Double Sharp and Double Flat Signs The Complete Major Chord Table. Interval Climbers (Octaves)	39
C and F Minor Scales and Chords	40
No. 9 Rockin' the Beat Along, Brandman	41
Left Hand Accompaniments	42
No. 10 Songbird, Brandman	43
The Minor Chord Table	44
No. 11 Night Flying, Brandman	45
Music Speed Reading: Root Position Tetrad Shapes and Octave Spans	46
Reading Intervals across the Great Staff. The Metronome (M.M.)	47
No. 12 Walkin' Easy, Brandman. Arpeggiando Sign	48
No. 13 Hava Nagila, arr. Brandman	50-51
Dominant Seventh Chords (F, C, G, D, A)	52
Ornaments. No. 14 Grasshopper Hop, Brandman. Acciaccatura	54
Pedalling	56
Pedalling Exercises	57
Chord and Pedal Study in D Major. Appoggiatura	58

No. 15 Falling Leaves, Brandman. Appoggiatura 59
Music Speed Reading: New Position Changing Methods Number Two
   Chord Climbing using Root Position Triads 60
No. 16 Old Dance Tune, Purcell 61
Chord Naming Systems No. 1 **Figured Bass** 62
Chord Naming Systems No. 2 **Modern Chord Symbols** 63
Music Speed Reading: Chord Climbing Exercises, First Inversion Triads 64
Wraggle Taggle Gypsies, O! When Johnny Comes Marching Home: Arranging 65
The Sound of Intervals 66
Music Speed Reading: Chord Climbing Exercises, Second Inversion Triads 67
Suspended Fourth Chords 68
Ostinato Bass 69
Trill. Repeat Bars 70
No. 17 The Rumble, Brandman 71
Position Changing 72
New Position Changing Methods No. 2 Helping Hand Exercises 73
Helping Hands – Left Hand Crossing Right 74
No. 18 Leaping Lizards, Brandman 75
Helping Hands – Right Hand Crossing Left 76
No. 19 Leaping Frogs, Brandman 77
Pedal Point 78
No. 20 Undercurrents, Brandman. Mordent 79
Jazz Timing. Boogie Woogie Left-Hand Patterns 80
The Blues Scale and Blues Notes 81
Improvising over a twelve-bar blues using a Boogie pattern
   and the Blues scale 82
F sharp and C sharp, Minor Scales and Chords 83
F and C Minor Contrary Motion Scales 84
No. 21 Go for Baroque, Brandman. Inverted Mordent 85
Music Speed Reading: Tetrad Shapes. Root, First and Second Inversion Shapes 86
No. 22 Minuet in G, Bach 87
Chord Progressions based on the Cycle of Fifths 88
Improvising on a chord pattern 89
New Position Changing Methods, Number Three.
   Shifting Shapes over the Interval of a Third 90
Shuffle Rhythm Patterns for Two Hands. Improvising Practice 91
No. 23 Sans Souci Shuffle, Brandman 92-93
Cadences 94
Playing Cadences 95-96
No. 24 Boogie Shake, Brandman. Tremolo 97
Diminished Seventh Chords 98
Chord Pattern 99
No. 25 On the Upturn, Brandman. Turn 100
Pictorial Patterns for Major Scales 102
Integrated Support Materials 103
Handy Manuscript Page 104

CONTEMPORARY PIANO METHOD
BOOK TWO
CONTENTS   PART   B

Modulation	111
No. 26 Gavotte, Handel	113
No. 27 Turn It Down, Brandman. Inverted Turn	115
Principles of Fingering	116
Tierce de Picardie	119
No. 28 Bateau Blue, Brandman. Speed Markings	120
Chords used for changes of sound colour	121
No. 29 Waltz for Kirk, Brandman. Swing Waltz	122
No. 30 Grecian Dance, Brandman. 7/4	123
B flat, E flat and A flat Minor scales and chords	124
Major Seventh Chords	126
Scale and Chord summary	127
No. 31 Sarabande, Handel	128
Chord Pattern using Major Sevenths. Suggested Practice Routine	129
Melodic Minor Scales. **A, E and B Minors**	130
Major Sixth and Minor Seventh Chords	131
Cycle progression	132
Rock Chord Pattern, Brandman, using Major Sixth chords	133
Country and Western playing style Major Scales over Two Octaves	134
No. 32 Roumanian Ride, Brandman. 7/8	135
D and G Melodic Minor Scales	137
Popular Dance Music of the Twentieth Century	138
The Tango, Brandman. Glissando	139
No. 33 Tango Azul, Brandman	140
Part Playing	141
C and F Melodic Minor Scales	143
No. 34 Sarabande, Buxtehude	144
Rock Chord Pattern using Major Sixths and Minor Sevenths	145
B flat, E flat and A flat Melodic Minor Scales	146
No. 35 Chacabuco, Cha Cha Cha Brandman	147-148

Minor Sixth and Minor Seventh Flattened Fifth
   (Half-Diminished Seventh) Chords..149
No. 36 Jucaro Rumba, Brandman..150-152
F sharp and C sharp Melodic Minor Scales..153
Cycle of Fifths...154
The Bossa Nova...155
No. 37 Bossa Nova de Bondi, Brandman..156
Improvising on a chord pattern...159
Swingin' in Style – chord pattern, Brandman...160
No. 38 Al's Café, Bailey..161-164
No. 39 Blueberry Ballad, Brandman...165
No. 40 Beneath the Coolabah Tree, Brandman...166
Crotchet Triplets..167
Crotchet Triplets continued and the Duplet..168
No. 41 Spiderswing, Brandman...169-172
Rhythmic Chord Patterns:
   Conga...173
   Motown...174
No. 42 Jingle Bells - disco/reggae arrangement, Brandman...175-176
No. 43 Benny's Beguine, Brandman...177
Rhythmic Chord Patterns: Jazz-Rock, Funk and Disco Patterns....................................179
No. 44 Funky Dancin', Brandman...181
Simple and Compound Intervals...184
No. 45 Sydney Samba, Brandman...186
No. 46 Make Mine Mambo, Brandman...189
No. 47 I'll Never Break Your Heart, Wilde and Manno – Popular Sheet Music............191
Advanced Modulation Spider Chart for Major Keys..196
Advanced Modulation Spider Chart for Minor Keys..197
Signs and Terms used in this Book..198
Suggested Practice Routine...199
Integrated Support Materials...200

MODULATION

To **Modulate** simply means to "change key". During the progress of many pieces of music, there are likely to be one or two, if not more, key changes. This is done by the addition of Sharps, Flats or Naturals written in the body of the music as Accidentals (i.e. NO change to the Key Signature at the beginning of the line).

Therefore when looking for a Modulation, find the added accidentals and assess whether they are only part of a Chromatic Scale or if they in fact, when added to the original Key Signature, indicate a new key.

In most Tonal music, that is music written in a Major or Minor Key, for instance popular songs and a large amount of Classical Music, the Modulation will be to a closely related key. These closely related Key centres all appear in the TABLE of chords. They are One sharp or One flat key either side of the Original Key Centre, in either the Major Form or the Relative Minor, not forgetting the relative of the original key centre.

When viewing the Modulation from the point of view of the Table, you can superimpose one Table over another. For instance:

(G TABLE)

IV	I	V
C	G	D
ii	vi	iii
Am	Em	Bm

(C TABLE)

IV	I	V
F	C	G
ii	vi	iii
Dm	Am	Em

If you view the Original Table as C Major, the KEY CENTRE has moved one position to the RIGHT to G Major, (one sharp more), OR if viewing the Original Table as G Major, we have moved one position to the LEFT, to C Major (one sharp less).

The chords that belong to both keys are PIVOT chords. These chords are the ones used to make the transition from one key to the other. Usually the Key change is then "clinched" by the use of the Dominant 7th of the Key or another chord that belongs ONLY to the NEW KEY.

If you can spot the Modulation, you will find it easier to remember the accidentals (which are really there on PURPOSE) as you will be thinking in the **scale and chords of the new key**, rather than trying to constantly alter the old key.

Another way to look at Modulation is using the Cycle of Fifths laid out in a straight line and using a "Slide Rule" effect.

Write out the Cycle thus:

Majors:	C♭	G♭	D♭	A♭	E♭	B♭	F	C	G	D	A	E	B	F♯	C♯	G♯
Minors:	A♭	E♭	B♭	F	C	G	D	A	E	B	F♯	C♯	G♯	D♯	A♯	E♯

Then take a piece of paper and cut a rectangular window large enough to see Three Majors and their Relative minors. See example 1.

Place the paper with the WINDOW over any three keys and as you move the paper to the left or to the right, the Table for the central letter will appear. If you are looking for the Closely related keys to the Minors just read the Table upside down with the Tonic (I) being the central letter on the lower line.

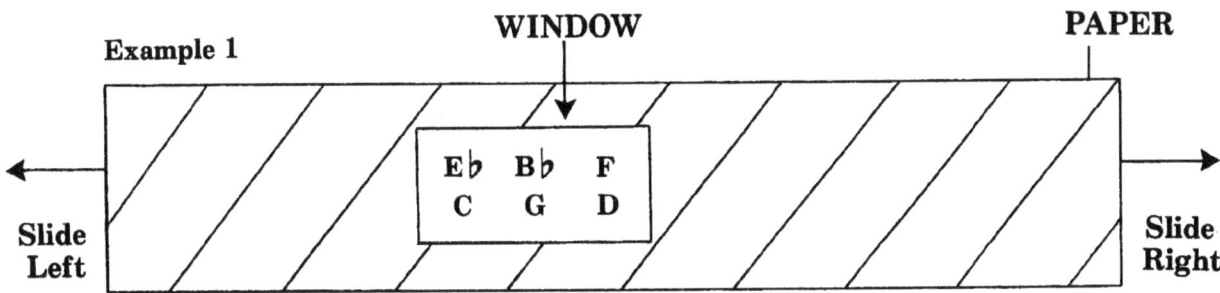

Chords that appear in both positions as you move the window are the Pivot Chords that are relevant to both keys.

MODULATION POINTS

Refer to Book 2 of the Contemporary Theory Workbook series, for the manner in which to set out the Modulation Points for each key. Draw a Modulation Point graph in a blank area on the page for each piece in this book. Then write full chord tables for the keys to which each piece modulates. For pieces which travel to all six keys, refer to the 'Modulation Spider' templates on pages 196 & 197. These can be photocopied and filled in for each key.

SPECIAL NOTE — MODULATION TO THE TONIC MINOR OR TONIC MAJOR KEY

Apart from the usual modulation points mentioned above, occasionally a composer may wish to impart a change of colour by modulating to the Tonic Major or Tonic Minor key. For Example, if the key of the piece is C Major the Modulation will be to C Minor or conversely if the key of the piece is C Minor the Modulation will be to C Major.

This is a fairly abrupt modulation owing to the fact that the tonality moves in one jump from the home key to one that is either three flats more or three sharps less, or vice-versa if starting on the Minor key. For Example from C Major (No sharps or flats) to C minor (3 Flats), B Major (5 sharps) to B Minor (2 sharps).

This sudden change in colour can alter the mood of the piece from the bright Major sound to the sombre Minor sound. It is often used very effectively. A traditional example can be found in the 15 Variations on the Eroica Theme and Fugue, Opus 35, by Ludwig Van Beethoven. The key of the entire work is E Flat Major (3 Flats). Variation 14 is in the Tonic Minor Key. E Flat Minor (6 Flats).

A more up-to-date example of this device can be found in the variations 'Sunshowers on the River' in the book 'Six Contemporary Piano Pieces' by the author.

113

Modulation Points

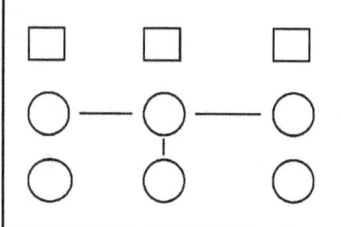

26. GAVOTTE

CHORD TABLES

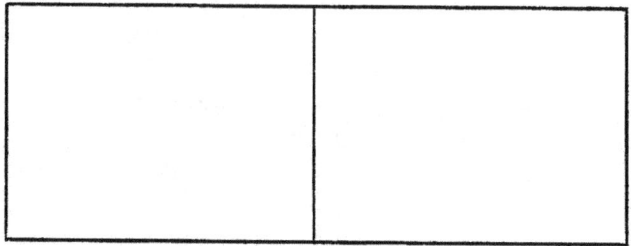

1. Indicate the Modulation and write the second table accordingly.
2. Write the Chord Names above each bar.
3. Name the Cadences marked: ⌐¬ 1. ....
   2. ....
   3. ....

This piece is in TERNARY form.
The middle section contrasts with
the first and last sections.
Mark the sections A. B. A.

GEORGE FREDERIC HANDEL, 1685-1759
German (lived also in England)
Baroque

INVERTED TURN

Take the **Keynote,** the note **below, Keynote,** the note **above** and return to the **Keynote.** N.B. The lower and upper notes must be taken from the scale unless otherwise indicated.

27. TURN IT DOWN!

WRITE CHORD TABLES IN THIS SPACE.

Piu — more. *Meno* — less.
Mosso — Movement or speed.

Piu Mosso = more speed (faster)
Meno Mosso = less speed (slower)

Andante Con Moto (with movement)

34321

PRINCIPLES OF FINGERING

When approaching a new piece of music, you usually have to find a suitable fingering to enable you to reach each note comfortably and move to new hand positions by feel whenever possible. A good approach to fingering is via the technical aspects learnt so far — scales, chords, etc.

1. The first method used is the **Five Finger Hand Position.** Scan through the music to see how many notes can be handled by one "5-finger" position. Often if there are one or two notes outside this position they can be handled by an **extension** of the five-finger position. That is, by stretching either the thumb or the fifth finger to cover the intervals of a sixth, seventh or octave, and/or by putting either the second or third finger over the thumb to handle one or two other notes of the scale. (See example 1a and 1b).

2. The next situation likely to occur is one where a **scale fingering** (i.e. a combination of two hand positions) is used. All the scales thus far learnt are likely to occur in the pieces you play. If you can identify the scale on the written music, you should then automatically know which fingers to use, through your previous study of the scale. Also do not forget the **Chromatic Scale fingering** for chromatic sections of the pieces you are playing. (See example 2).

3. The third type of situation likely to occur in your pieces is that of either **block** or **broken chords.** The fingering for these and all of their inversions should be part of your automatic memory bank, if they have been well practised. Also keep in mind that the chords may be 3, 4 or 5 note chords. (Dom. 7th etc). The 5-note fingering is similar to that of Arpeggios in that the hand is usually stretched over an octave span with one finger on each note of the chord. (See example 3).

4. **Arpeggio** fingerings for three and four note chords will be dealt with in Book Three. The basic idea of an Arpeggio is that of a chord that repeats itself (in broken form of course) over several octaves. (See example 4).

5. **Other methods of changing position.** (a) If you have to move into the next octave, a common method of changing position is to swap fingers on one note without re-striking it. To go up, using the right hand, hold the 5th finger down and swap to the thumb. Reverse the process to go down. This method holds good for position changes over any other interval up to an octave as well.

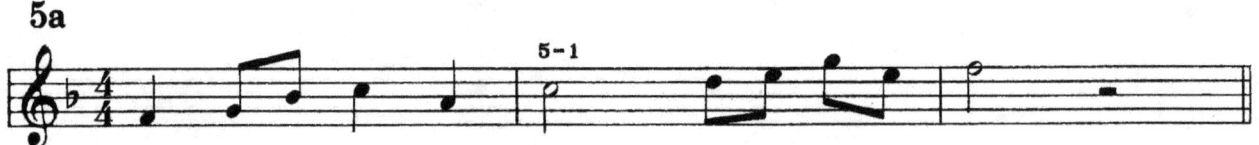

5.(b) Another good place to change hand position is on a repeated note. This gives you a chance to finish off one area in one hand position and set yourself up for a new area on the same note. (The Technique of changing the fingers on repeated notes, should be borne in mind for extended sections of rapidly repeated notes).

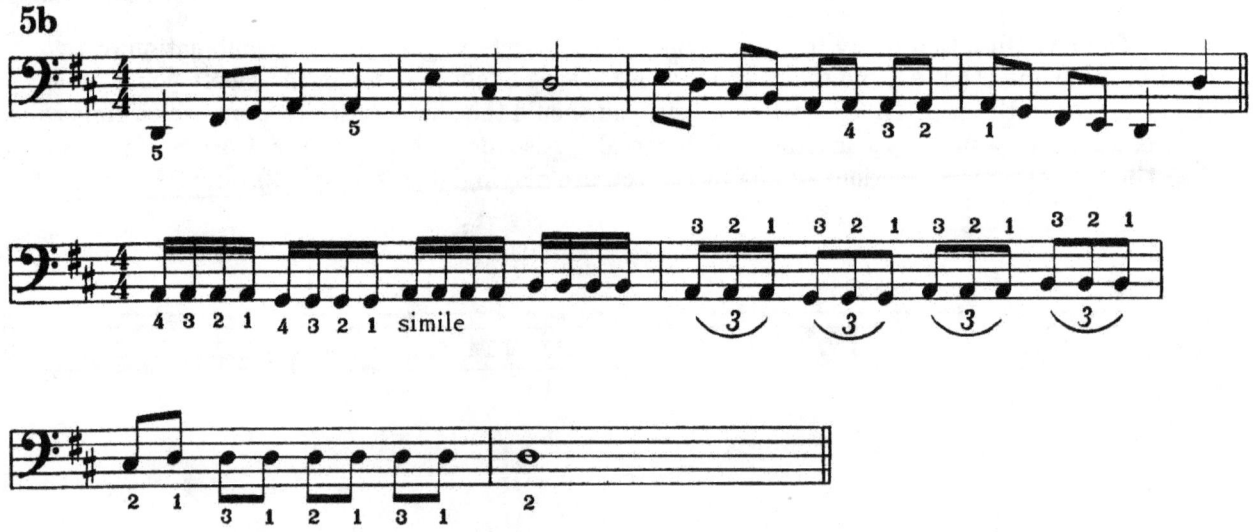

5.(c) Shifting the Hand Position up a step (2nd) or down a step as in the Interval and Chord Climbing Exercises. (See pages 60, 64 and 67).

5.(d) Using a Helping Hand. Take your bearings for the new position from one hand or the other, e.g. if the Right Hand is retaining the position, the Left Hand can cross over it and take the new position in relation to the Right Hand note. (See pages 72 — 77).

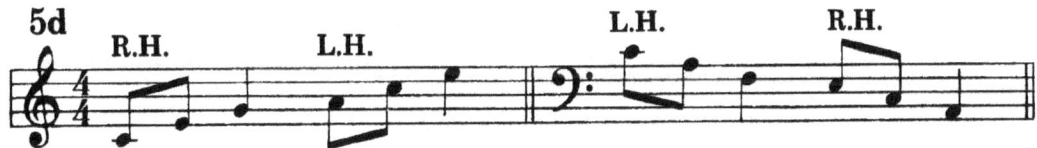

5.(e) Shifting the Hand Position Up or Down by the distance of a Skip (3rd) by skimming the fingers lightly over the keys. (See page 93).

5(f) Contraction of the Hand. The hand can be contracted so that the fingers are brought closer together, and can be lined up over a new set of notes.

Summary

1. (a) Five-finger Hand-Position (b) with extensions.
2. Scale Fingerings — All Major and Minor and Chromatic.
3. Chord Fingerings 3, 4 and 5-note chords, Block and Broken and inversions.
   (Including Positions based on the octave).
4. Arpeggio Fingerings.
5. Methods of changing Position.

Further thoughts on fingering

Always tailor your fingering to the specific situation. If you are doing a scale and chord analysis for all the pieces that you are playing, this will facilitate the finding of appropriate fingering for all these aspects of your music. You will then find that you only have to indicate the "Key" fingering for a section of music, rather than writing all the fingering numbers above all the notes. (The "Key" fingering is one that indicates a hand position; for instance — the number 3 over the note "E" would indicate a five finger position over the notes C, D, E, F and G).

This process then cleans up the page and leaves your eyes and mind free to concentrate on the intervals and the fingers free to concentrate on feel. It also means that you do not have to "sift" through the mass of fingerings on the page to find out which ones are really important in relation to a change of position. (At all other times you should be reading intervals!). I suggest that you use a typing correction fluid to block out the unnecessary fingering on the printed music. If you can work out a more logical fingering than suggested by the editor of the pieces you are studying, by all means block out the printed fingering and substitute your own "Key" fingerings on the music.

TIERCE de PICARDIE (Picardie Third)

This is the practice of ending a piece of music in a Minor key on the Tonic Major chord. The Oxford Companion to Music says: "This idiom was common in the sixteenth and seventeenth centuries and the beginning of the eighteenth century. It was felt to be unsuitable to bring the changing harmonies to rest on the interval of a minor third, since keen ears could detect the major third occurring as one of the harmonics of the keynote."

The fifth harmonic in the series is the Major Third and under certain circumstances, for instance in a large Gothic Cathedral, this harmonic can be heard very predominantly due to the acoustics of the hall. Thus if the choir singing in a large Cathedral sang the final long Minor Chord of a work, there would be a clash between the Minor Third Interval being sung and the Major Third Harmonic resonating through the Church.

The Oxford Companion says that: "Most probably the name has something to do with the high development of contrapuntal choral music in the North of France and Flanders in the fifteenth century." (Picardie is in Northern France).

The effect of the Major Triad at the end of a Minor piece is that of refreshing brightness and the feeling of calm resolution. Listen to the effect in the following piece and judge for yourself.

For more information on the Harmonic Series refer to the Contemporary Chord Workbook Book 2 by the author.

THE SOFT PEDAL

The Italian term used to denote the Soft Pedal is "Una Corda" which literally means that only one string should sound, although in practice on a Grand Piano two strings sound when this pedal is depressed, instead of the usual three strings. This occurs when the action of the piano moves to the Right as the pedal is depressed.

On an upright model the hammers move closer to the keys, thereby producing a softer sound.

As mentioned previously, the hammer usually hits three strings when the soft pedal is released. Therefore the Italian term to denote the release of the Soft Pedal is "Tre Corde" (three strings). At the beginning of this piece, both the sustain pedal and the soft pedal are used simultaneously.

28. BATEAU BLUE

CHORD TABLES

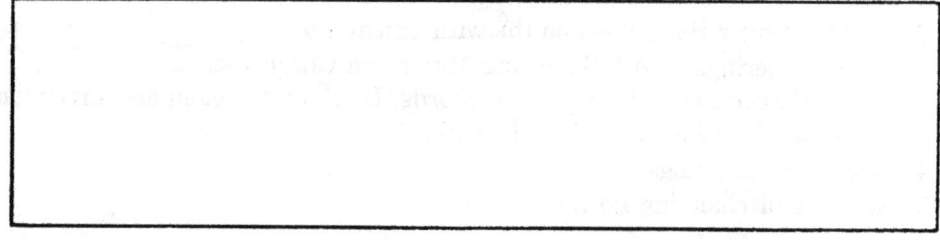

Accelerando (Accel) — gradually getting faster.
Ritardando (Rit) and *Rallentando (Rall)* gradually getting slower.
Ritenuto (Riten) — Immediately slower.

Write in the Chord names above the bars.

CHORDS USED FOR CHANGES OF SOUND COLOUR

There are two chords commonly used to give changes of colour to the sound of a piece. They are (1) the Minor Chord used on the IVth degree of a piece in a Major Key, and (2) the Augmented Chord used on the Vth degree of both a Major or Minor Piece.

MINOR CHORD USED ON IV

If a piece were in the key of G Minor and used the chords iv to I as the final Cadence (ending formula) making the last chord a Major chord (Tierce De Picardie) those two chords would be Cm (iv) to G (I).

This same sound is often used in pieces in a Major Key. (Having established a mixture of Major and Minor chords in compositions which finished with a Tierce De Picardie, it became easy to transfer the sound to pieces in Major Keys). Many composers of the later 19th Century used this sound to colour their music in the search for something a little different.

The use of chords with altered notes from the Key Signature, known as Chromatic chords, was a common feature of music of the 19th Century. Keep in mind that this chord is likely to occur in many pieces, especially ballads. It adds a melancholy quality to the harmony of the song or piece.

AUGMENTED CHORD USED ON V

Another chord which is used to colour the harmony of many pieces is the Augmented chord. (See page 38). As it has a strong leading sound it is used on the Vth degree of the scale as a variation of the Dominant Triad. Also the Dominant Seventh chord is often used with an Augmented 5th as well. The combination of both the Dominant Seventh note and the Augmented Fifth notes in the same chord provides a very strong pull. Note that in the Minor Chord Table, the notes of the Augmented triad on the **third degree** are the same as those in the Augmented version of the Dominant triad.

Play and listen to the sound of these chords and a progression of chords such as I ii V+ I.

ADDITIONS TO THE TABLE OF CHORDS

Mark in these two possibilities on the Major Table by placing a small "iv" above the IV and by placing a small plus sign (+) above the V, as shown below.

Use only the plus sign (+) above the V for the Minor Chord Table.

MAJOR CHORD TABLE

(iv)		(+)
IV	I	V
ii	vi	iii
		vii°

MINOR CHORD TABLE

		(+)
iv	i	V
VI	III	ii°
		vii°

29. WALTZ FOR KIRK

CHORD TABLES

Write the Chord names in above each bar.
Swing Waltz — Allegretto

30. GRECIAN DANCE

Complete the Chord Table and write the chord names above the bars. Note the Left Hand chord shapes (three-note or four-note shapes) and finger them accordingly. For example Bar 5 can be seen as a four-note shape, and fingering it as such means that less hand movement is involved. Consequently it becomes easier to play, particularly if you want to play the piece at speed.

CHORD TABLES

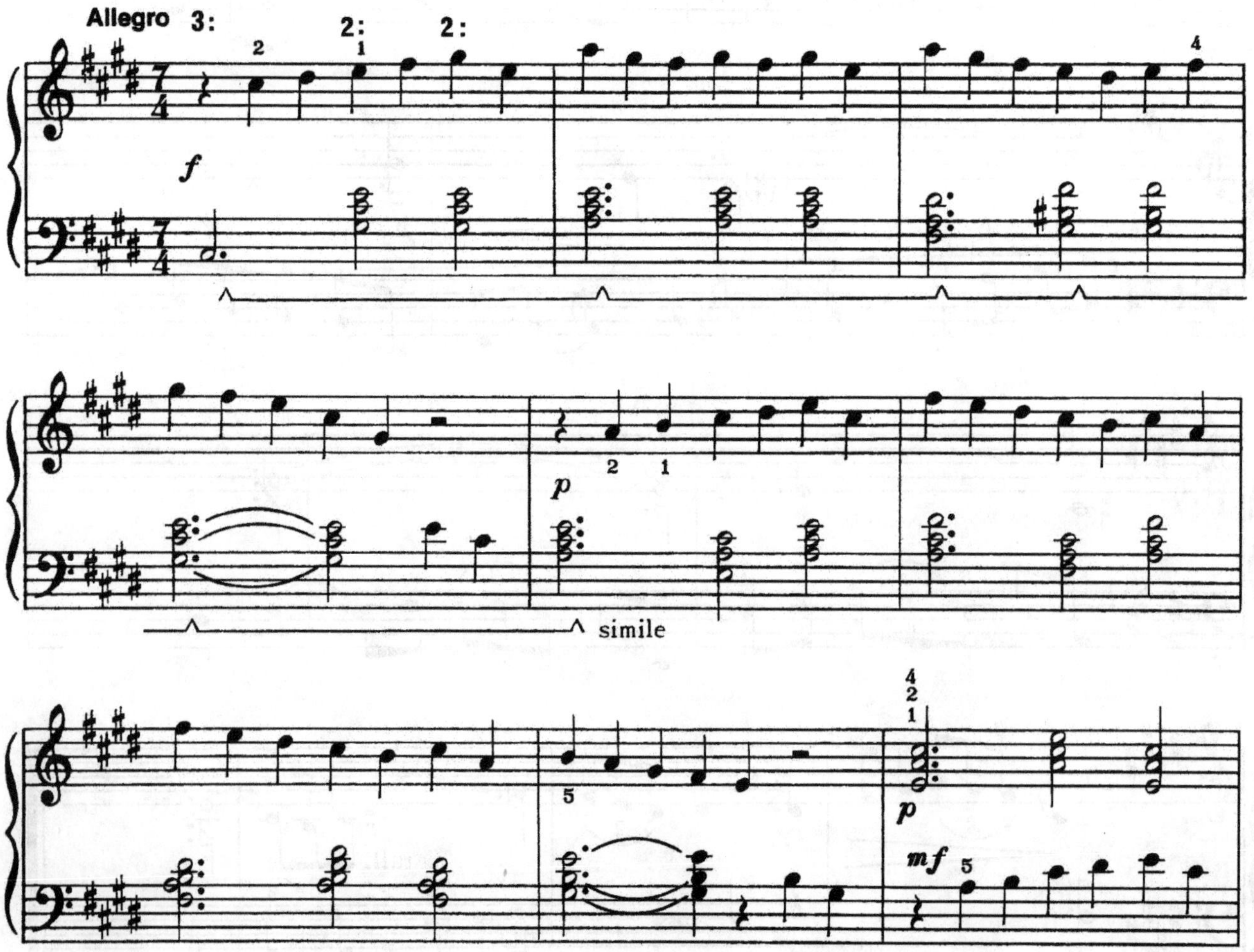

B FLAT, E FLAT AND A FLAT HARMONIC MINOR SCALES

The last three minor harmonic scales to be introduced are B Flat, E Flat and A Flat minors. B Flat and E Flat minors can be regarded as a set according to the fingering and A Flat minor really belongs with F sharp and C sharp Minors from the fingering point of view.

B FLAT MINOR

B Flat Minor is related to D Flat Major and therefore has 5 Flats: B, E, A, D and G. The only white notes played in the natural minor form are F and C. The Right Hand Fingering is 2 1 2 3 1 2 3 4 and the Left Hand Fingering is 2 1 3 2 1 4 3 2. When the 7th is raised in the Harmonic Form the same fingering is used even though the seventh is raised from the black note A Flat to the white note A Natural.

E FLAT MINOR

E Flat Minor being related to G Flat Major has 6 Flats: B, E, A, D, G and C. When the Natural Minor is played, the only white notes are F and C Flat (B white note). The fingering is R.H. 2 1 2 3 4 1 2 3 and L.H. 2 1 4 3 2 1 3 2. The fingering is exactly the same for the Harmonic Form when the 7th is raised from D Flat to D Natural. NOTICE that in both B Flat and E Flat Minor Scales the left hand fingering finishes 3 2.

A FLAT MINOR

A Flat Minor scale is the last Minor key in the cycle of 5ths to be covered in my system. As it is related to C Flat Major it has 7 flats: B, E, A, D, G, C and F, and as there are only 7 different notes in a scale just flatten each one. Play the Natural Minor with the right hand saying as you go — A Flat, B Flat, C Flat, D Flat, E Flat, F Flat, G Flat, A Flat. The R.H. fingering is 3 4 1 2 3 1 2 3 (the same as F sharp and C sharp Minors). The only white notes are C Flat & F Flat. Next play the Harmonic Minor in the R.H. with the 7th raised from G Flat to G Natural. The fingering is the same as the Natural Minor form. The Left Hand should then play the Harmonic Form with this fingering: 3 2 1 4 3 2 1 3 (the same as C sharp Harmonic Minor). You will find that the Natural Minor fingering has to be 3 2 1 3 2 1 4 3 for the L.H.

MINOR CHORDS

The three new Minor chords from these scales are of course **B Flat Minor** — B♭, D♭ and F, **E Flat Minor** — E♭, G♭ and B♭, and **A Flat Minor** — A♭, C♭ and E♭. Play them all in inversions in block and broken forms.

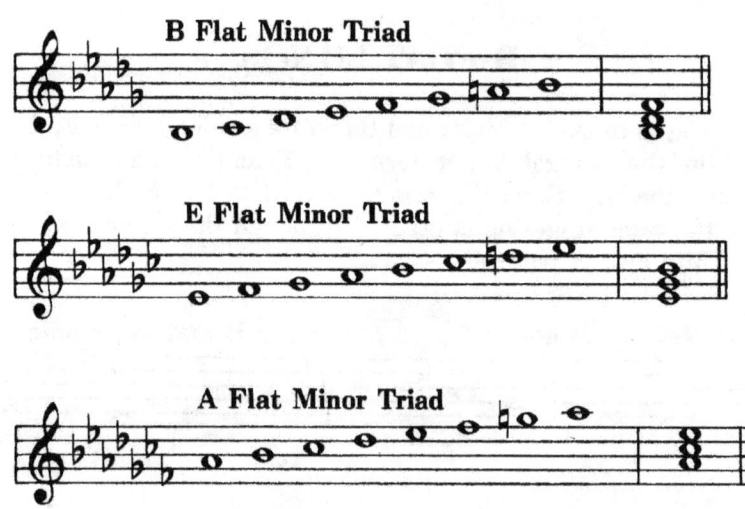

CONTRARY MINOR SCALES

At this stage we can move on to F sharp and C sharp contrary minor scales. Play the right hand up and back first then the left hand down and up. Do not forget to stretch the tone and a half from the 7th down to the 6th degrees in the left hand. In both these scales they are white notes: in F sharp minor, 7 down to 6 = E sharp to D, and in C sharp minor 7 down to 6 = B sharp to A. In C sharp Minor the trick is to remember the three white notes: B sharp which falls the same time as a black note in the opposite hand and A and E white notes which fall together. If you find similar clues for all the contrary scales they will be easier to remember.

Major 7th Chords

If you refer back to page 52 under the heading Dominant 7th Chords, you will recall that a "7th" chord can be built on each note of the Major Scale. The 7th chord built on the TONIC (1st degree) is therefore the TONIC 7th and it is this chord that is known in popular music as the Major 7th Chord.

These chords are very easy to build. Just take the Major Triad on the 1st degree and add the seventh note of the Major scale to it. For instance, take C chord, (C, E, G), and add the seventh note of C scale (B), to it. Thus C Major seventh is C, E, G and B; G Major Seventh is G, B, D and F sharp; D Major Seventh is D and F sharp, A and C sharp, and so on. The distances between each of the notes of the chord are, in semitones — 4:3:4.

These chords are rest chords and therefore very good final chords for a tune, whereas the previously learnt Dominant and Diminished 7th chords both perform leading functions. Learn all the Major 7th chords in the Cycle of Fifths. Practise them in inversions in the form given for Dominant sevenths on page 53. Do not forget the Broken Chord Forms as well.

CONTRARY MINORS

The last three contrary minors to learn are B♭, E♭ and A♭ Harmonic Minors. In B♭ Minor remember that the three white notes are C, F and A. Play the scale, hands separately; right hand up and down and left hand, down and up. Also remember to begin the left hand descending form with fingers 2-3-4. The clue to remembering this scale is that the white notes A and C occur at the same time and the F occurs at the same time as the black note E Flat.

In E Flat Minor also, remember that the left hand descending fingering begins 2-3-1. The white notes D and F occur at the same time and C Flat (B white note) falls at the same time as G Flat in the opposite hand.

In A Flat Minor, the white note G falls at the same time as B Flat in the other hand and F Flat (white note E) occurs with C Flat (white note B). The white notes in this scale make up the shape of an E minor chord. Look at the other Contrary Motion Scales so far covered to see what other chord shapes are created by the white notes of the scale.

SCALE AND CHORD SUMMARY

Here is a Summary of all chords and scales covered up to this point. The Similar Motion scales you should be playing are: Majors D Flat, A Flat, E Flat, B Flat, F, C, G, D, A, E, B and F Sharp. (One octave) Harmonic and Natural Minors: A Flat, E Flat, B Flat, F, C, G, D, A, E, B, F Sharp and C Sharp (one octave).

You should also be playing the respective Major and Minor Triads (as 3 and 4-note chords) and the respective Major and Harmonic Minor Contrary Motion Scales.

Other chords already covered in this course are all Diminished, Augmented and Suspended 4th Triads and all the Dominant Seventh, Diminished Seventh and the above Major Seventh Chords.

As well, you should be playing the Chromatic Scale over a distance of two octaves from any starting note.

31. SARABANDE

Study the Left Hand part carefully, in order to decide whether the notes belong to three or four-note chord shapes. Finger them accordingly.

Clap the timing of each separate
stave before playing this piece.

CHORD TABLES

SARABANDE

Write the Chord names above the bars.

GEORGE FREDERIC HANDEL

Lento — Slowly

SUGGESTED PRACTICE ROUTINE

A Suggested Practice Routine: As the summary on page 127 represents quite a deal of material to be learnt and remembered, it is quite helpful to practise all this technical work on a rotation system. I suggest taking 5 Major Keys and 5 Minor Keys each day and practising all forms of scales chords in these 5 Keys only, for the day. For instance, on Monday: C, G, D, A and E; on Tuesday: B, F sharp, D Flat, A Flat and E Flat; on Wednesday: B Flat, F, C, G and D; and so on around the Cycle of Fifths. You will observe that by taking 5 Keys each day's combination is different.

The value of this system, apart from the time saving, is that you will have a chance to concentrate your energies on these five keys and sort out the problems, rather than feeling you have to play every scale every day. As these scales become more fluent and naturally a little faster you will then leave some time to handle the new material as it is added.

CHORD PATTERN

1. The following is a Broken Chord accompaniment pattern on the types of chord so far learnt. Similar figures would be suitable as accompaniments to tunes such as "If" by David Gates, "My Way" by Paul Anka or "The Way We Were" as performed by Barbra Streisand.

Play the example as written. Then:

2. Play the chords in the Left Hand in quavers in the Broken chord style shown, and supply your own improvised Right Hand melody.

N.B. E♭/B♭ means E Flat Major Chord over a B Flat Bass Note.

MELODIC MINOR SCALES

Up to this stage we have covered all the Major and Minor Keys. Previously, I mentioned that there were 3 forms of the Minor Scale — Natural, Harmonic and Melodic. Please refer to page 18 for the details. So far we have learnt the Harmonic Forms via the Natural Minor Forms and in this way become familiar with all the Minor Keys. Now you can learn the Melodic Form, also via the Natural Minor Form, and you should have no problem grasping the Melodic Form now that the Major and Minor Key relationships are learnt and understood.

The first set of three scales comprises A, E and B Melodic Minors.

A MELODIC MINOR SCALE

The pattern is set by "A" Melodic Minor. Remembering that A Minor is related to C Major: play the Natural Minor form (no sharps or flats), then from there raise (sharpen) both the 6th and 7th degrees in the ascending scale and lower (naturalise) them in the descending scale.

Thus the pattern has two black notes together on the way up and those same degrees are white notes on the way back. (In the case of A Minor they are F sharp and G sharp ascending and F Natural and G Natural descending).

E MELODIC MINOR

Apply this pattern to E Minor (related to G Major, 1 sharp = F sharp). Play the Natural Minor first then raise the 6th and 7th degrees to C sharp and D sharp ascending and lower them back again to C and D Naturals in the descending form.

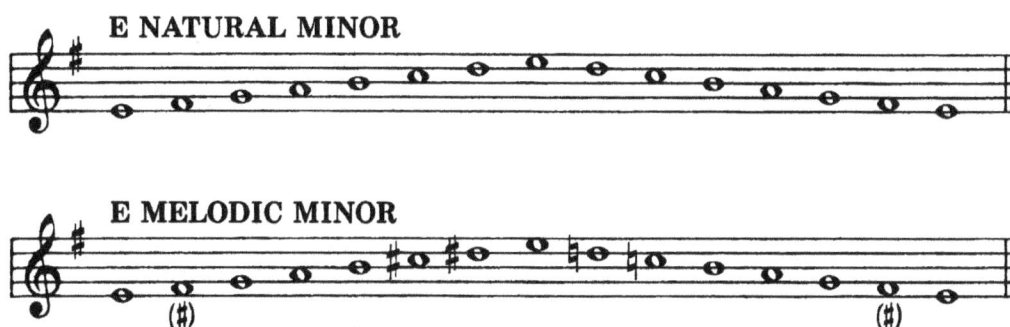

B MELODIC MINOR

B Minor is related to D Major (2 sharps = F and C). After playing the natural form, play the Melodic form by raising the 6th and 7th to G sharp and A sharp ascending, and lowering them to G and A naturals descending. (Do not forget that the Left Hand Fingering is 4 3 2 1 4 3 2 1).

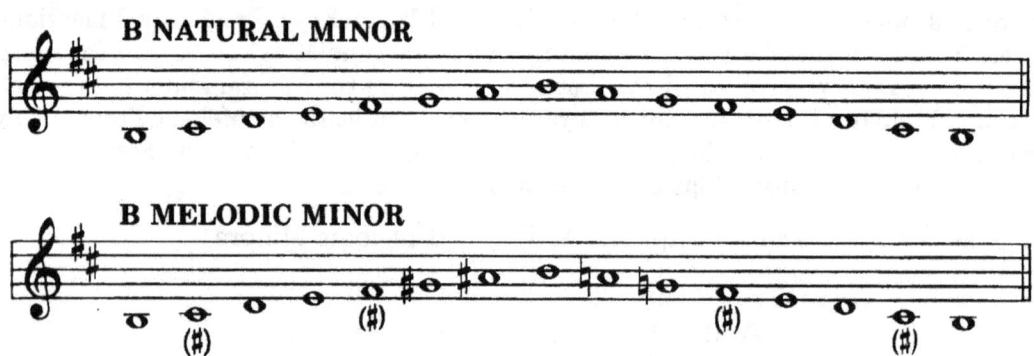

MAJOR 6TH AND MINOR 7TH CHORDS

Another type of chord found in the Major Scale is the Major 6th chord. If you take the Major Triad on the Tonic degree of the scale and add the sixth note of the scale to it you will have built a Major 6th Chord. (In Classical terminology they are known as "Added 6th Chords"). Thus C Major 6th consists of C, E, G and A. The Major 6th would be a good final chord in a piece in a Major Key.

It is a curious fact that when you reach the Third inversion of this chord, it becomes the Minor 7th chord on the 6th degree (A), i.e. A, C, E and G.

Note that the triad is minor and that the added seventh is the Flattened seventh from A. This chord therefore will occur in a Major Key functioning as either the 6th degree or the 2nd degree (or possibly the 3rd degree also) Seventh, rather than as the 1st degree chord in a minor Key. The reason I mentioned the 2nd and 3rd degree 7ths as well is that in construction they are also minor 7ths. (See page 52).

Thus in a Cycle of Fifths progression in C Major the following chords could be played instead of simple triads: C6(I), Emi7(III), Ami7(VI), Dmi7(II), G7(V) and C6(I).

PRACTISE THE CHORD IN BOTH FORMS. Separate hands and hands together.

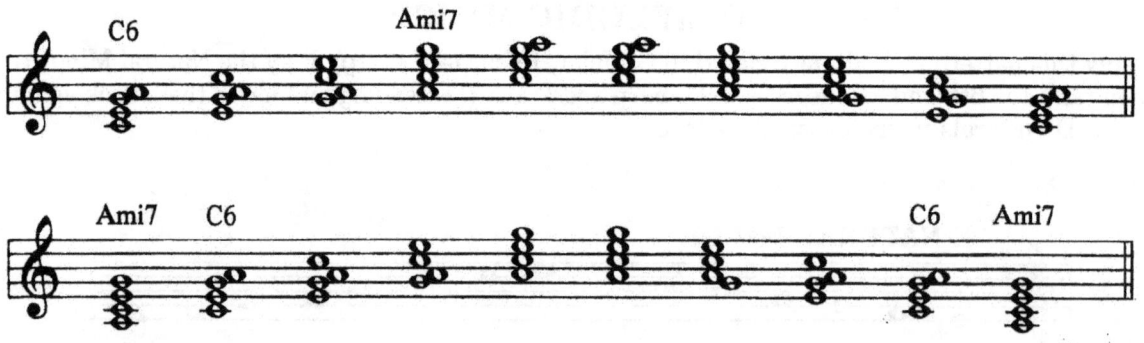

Learn the Major 6ths and their corresponding Minor Sevenths on the notes F, C, G, D, A, E and B. (The Minor sevenths will be, in order, D, A, E, B, F sharp and C sharp, and G sharp min7ths).

CYCLE PROGRESSIONS

Many pieces, both classical and modern, make use of progressions moving anti-clockwise around the Cycle of Fifths. (See the vi ii V I progression discussed on page 88). Below are some suggestions as to how to practise the progressions, using (a) Dominant 7th moving to Tonic Triad (b) Dominant 7th moving to Tonic Major 6th chord and (c) a handy Left Hand pattern which implies the Dominant 7th and Tonic triads by using the intervals of a Minor 7th and Major 3rd respectively. This last pattern can be filled out by the use of triads, sevenths or sixth chords in the Right Hand.

(1) Play hands separately, then hands together. Play the unit an octave higher than written when using the Left Hand. Also start a similar pattern on the F7 chord so that all chord shapes are covered and practise similar patterns beginning on a different inversion of the first chord each time, keeping each subsequent chord in the closest inversion to the preceding chord.

For more chord progression suggestions, refer to page 40 of
Pictorial Patterns for Keyboard Scales and Chords (Brandman)

CHORD PATTERN

The following chord pattern is another variation of the 12-bar Blues chord sequence. The Right Hand figure is a typical "Rock" figure characteristic of many Rock tunes of the 1960's. The Left Hand has a "Walking Bass" line constructed from the notes of the chords.

Practise playing the Major 6th chords, Dominant Seventh chords and Diminished Seventh chords and use them in this chord pattern.

Transpose the pattern to all 12 Major Keys.

Keep in mind that all 'Rock' Music is played with a 'Straight Eight' (straight quaver) feel, unless it is marked Shuffle, Swing or Jazz Feel.

Therefore, for Rock music simply count 1 + 2 + 3 + 4 + in each bar.

COUNTRY AND WESTERN

This style of music has its origins in the early cowboy songs of the American west and is also heavily influenced by Negro Blues and Shuffle feels, although there are differences from region to region. Similar developments have occurred in this style of music in Australia through the influence of radio and television. Tamworth, New South Wales, is the Australian capital of Country and Western music.

Nashville, U.S.A., which has always been considered the American capital of Country and Western, has seen many Blues and Jazz musicians lend their sound to the style.

The Floyd Cramer style of Piano 'lick', with its many Grace notes that emulate the sliding sound of the Pedal Steel Guitar, which is played with a metal bar known also as a 'steel' or 'Bottleneck', typifies the C&W sound found in most of the music.

Refer to *Pictorial Patterns for Keyboard Scales and Chords* pages 18-29 for graphics of all Major and Minor scales over the two octave range.

MAJOR SCALES — 2 OCTAVES

By this time in your learning programme, you probably know the Major Scales reasonably well. So why not try to extend the range of C and G Majors, firstly and then when you have the hang of those, apply the pattern to D, A and E Majors as well.

To play C Major over two octaves, play the first seven degrees in the Right Hand and then replace the fifth finger on top C with the thumb and simply repeat the pattern for the first octave. In the descending form remember that the 4th finger falls on the note "B" only and the other fingers will fall naturally into place. Likewise for the Left Hand remember that the 4th finger falls on the note "D" only and the other fingers will fall into place. Similarly, look for the 4th finger spots in G, D, A and E major scales if you want to play them over 2 octaves.

As an added note to this subject, once you have mastered two-octave scales you will easily be able to extend them to three and four octaves by repeating the pattern.

C MAJOR SCALE — Compass: Two Octaves.

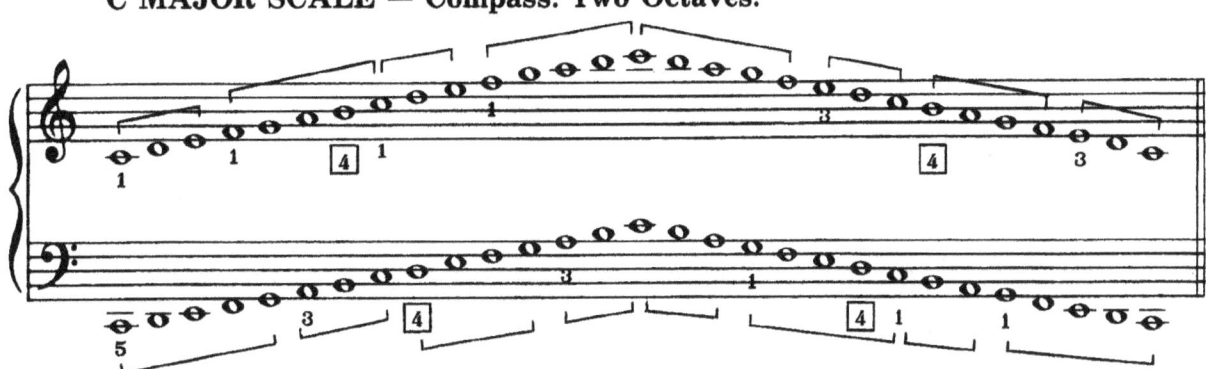

MAJOR SCALES — 2 OCTAVES

If you are comfortable with the pattern given on page 134 for the two-octave scales of C, G, D, A and E Majors, add the Majors of F and B in two-octave form to them. Check for "4th" finger spots in both scales. If they are correct everything else will fall into place.

R.H.: F Major — 4 on every B Flat (and F to finish); B Major — 4 on A Sharp only.

L.H.: F Major — 4 on G only; B Major — 4 on B to start, then F Sharps only.

32. ROUMANIAN RIDE

DYNAMIC MARKINGS

Supply your own dynamic markings (*f. p. cresc. dim.* etc.) to this piece. Keep in mind that usually an ascending figure is played with a crescendo and a descending figure is played with a diminuendo.

When you have decided on the dynamic levels and the graduations, write in the markings on the appropriate place on the page.

COLOUR AND CLAP

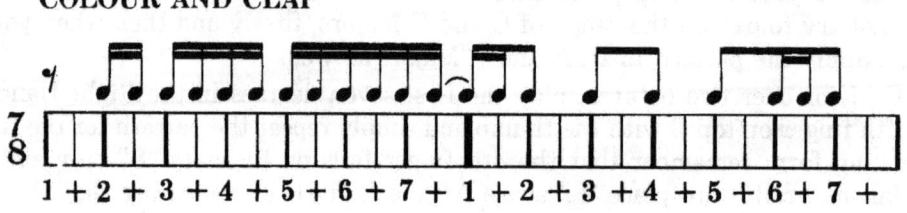

CHORD TABLES

ROUMANIAN RIDE

D AND G MELODIC MINOR SCALES

D MELODIC MINOR

D and G Melodic Minors can be regarded as a set. After playing the Natural Minor form of D with one Flat, B Flat (relative to F Major), raise the 6th and 7th degrees to B Natural and C Sharp in the ascending scale and lower them to C Natural and B Flat, (just like the Natural Minor), in the descending scale. Check back to page 18 if you cannot remember the theory behind the scale form.

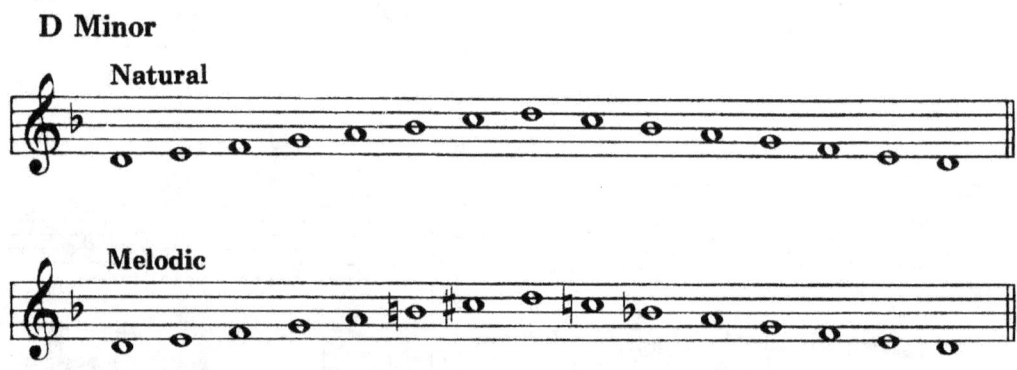

G MELODIC MINOR

G Minor (two flats — B and E, relative to B Flat Major) is very similar to D Melodic Minor. After playing the Natural Minor form, repeat the scale raising the 6th and 7th degrees to E Natural and F Sharp in the ascending form and lowering them to F Natural and E Flat in the descending form. Notice that both these scales finish with a similar pattern on the keyboard, i.e. Ascending: White (6), Black (7), White (8), and descending: White (8), White (7) and Black (6).

The fingering for these two scales is exactly the same as for the scales of G and D Major.

POPULAR DANCE MUSIC OF THE TWENTIETH CENTURY

The ballroom dance music of the twentieth century stems from the English Ballroom-dancing tradition. The forerunners to the Modern Dances were the nineteenth century dances such as Polka, Waltz, Cakewalk, Galop, etc.

At an **"Old-time"** dance, such pattern dances as the "Pride of Erin" (bright 3/4), the "Gypsy Tap" (bright 2/4), "La Bomba" (4/4 with a similar rhythm to the Tango), the "Maxina" (Medium 4/4), "Swing Waltz" (bright 3/4) and the "Barn Dance" (4/4, 3/4, 6/8 and 2/4 versions) are still danced.

These dances involve a certain set cycle of steps which repeat over a 32 or 24 bar pattern and in several of the dances the female dancers move from one partner to the other around the dancing circle, in what is known as a "Progressive" version of the dance. The music must therefore adhere strictly to the set number of bars.

The "Modern Dance"

In the Modern Dance the number of bars is not crucial although the correct tempo is. Two well-known modern dances which were formulated in the 1920's are the Slow Foxtrot, later simply known as the Foxtrot, and the Quick Foxtrot, later known as the Quickstep. The Foxtrot is written in Common Time (4/4) and the recommended speed is M.M. ♩ = 120. The Quickstep is usually written in Cut Common Time (2/2) (Alla Breve Time) and the recommended speed is M.M. ♩ = 200.

The other modern dance is the Jazz Waltz (recommended speed M.M. ♩ = 90). This is a slower version of the Waltzes danced at the Old-Time dances.

LATIN-AMERICAN DANCE MUSIC

From the early years of the twentieth century, many of the dances of central and south America were imported to the United States and England and incorporated into the ballroom dancing repertoire under the combined heading of *Latin-American* dance music.

The first of the dances to arrive was the TANGO, which was brought to New York in 1911 in a stage production: "Review of 1911" and became all the rage by 1914. Other dances followed, the RUMBA which was popular in the United States in 1929, the SAMBA, popular in the late 1930's, MAMBO, BEGUINE, CONGA and later the CHA CHA CHA (1962) and BOSSA NOVA.

Another dance which was added to the repertoire was the *Paso Doble* which is mainly danced by professional ballroom dancers at exhibitions. The dance is of Spanish origin and the movements are symbolic of those made by the Torero (or Matador) in the bull-ring. The lady presents her cape with movements suggestive of the Cape passes made by the Bull fighter.

The Jitterbug dance which was danced to the Boogie-Woogie music of the 1940's was modified in the 1950's to become the JIVE which is now thought of as a standard dance in the Latin-American group. From the Jive, the Rock and Roll style of dancing was developed. This style is similar to the Jive but is simpler and less energetic than the Jive.

In the 1960's the Twist arrived followed by the free-for-all styles of self-expression that were danced to Disco music and its offshoots.

THE TANGO

The word Tango is of Negro origin, formed in imitation of the drum beat with an accent on the second syllable, Tangó.

The Argentine Tango which is found in the vicinity of Buenos Aires, has a common rhythmic figure with the *Habanera*. According to the Argentine music scholar, Carlos Vega, the Habanera can be traced to the Country Dance of seventeenth century England. The English Country Dance became the French "Contradanse" which was then imported to Spain and known as the "Contradanza" or simply "Danza".

When imported to Cuba by the Spaniards it became the "Danza Habanera", that is, the "dance of Havana". The dance was then reintroduced to Spain as the "Habanera". During the Spanish-American war (c1900) a version of the Habanera, known as the Habanera del Cafe, appeared. It was this dance which became the forerunner of the Argentine Tango.

The most well-known example of a Habanera is the one from Bizet's Carmen. According to the researcher Nicholas Slominsky,* the tune was not written by Bizet, but borrowed from a song called "El Areglito" by the Spanish Composer Sebastian Yradier and published with the subtitle Chanson Havanaise.

There are two rhythms used for the Tango depending on whether the Tango style is more like the Habanera (Spanish Tango) or the later Argentine Tango.

*Nicholas Slonimsky, *Music of Latin-America*, Pub. Thomas Y. Crowell Company, New York, 1945.

GLISSANDO

The sign for a Glissando is: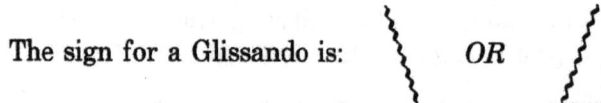

Often "gliss" is written next to it. It means to glide lightly over the white keys from the first written note to the second, sounding each note briefly as the finger glides over it.

To play a descending Glissando with the Right Hand, turn the hand to the side so that it is possible to glide down the keyboard on the thumb nail. Take care to play lightly so that no damage is done to they skin on the edge of the thumb nail.

To play an ascending Glissando, with the Right Hand, turn the hand to the side with the palm facing upwards, so that the finger nails of the middle three fingers are touching the keys. Glide up on the nail of the middle finger or if you like on the nails of the three middle fingers.

For the Left Hand use the thumb nail to ascend and the middle finger nail to descend.

Sometimes a glissando can be played on the black keys. It is more difficult but it can best be done by using the flat of the hand with the wrist turned to the side.

PART PLAYING

In many pieces a single hand may have to play two parts (i.e. two melodic lines). It is useful to practise some of the finger exercises given below so that the hands will be able to play the figures found in many pieces, with ease.

Baroque music, the European and English music of 1650 to 1750, was composed with the idea of two or more voices or parts moving simultaneously. The word Polyphonic (from Poly meaning "many" and Phon meaning "voice" or "sound") is used to describe this music. The style of the music is often also described as Contrapuntal meaning two or more voices set in contrast to each other, (point against point).

The instrumental music was styled largely on vocal music which, by its very nature of each person being only able to sing one part or voice, was Contrapuntal. The keyboard instruments of the day, the Harpsichord and Clavichord (the piano had not been invented), did not have the advantage of the "Sustain" Pedal so any parts that had to be sustained had to be held by the fingers.

You will find many instances of this type of writing in the music of J. S. Bach, particularly the "3-Part Inventions" and the Preludes and Fugues, and in the music of Handel, Scarlatti and other Baroque composers.

Most keyboard music from the Baroque period onwards employs at least small sections of part playing. The technique is particularly useful if one wishes to play both the melody and accompaniment in one hand in a Rhumba or Beguine for instance. (See page 151).

Note the 4th finger crossing over the 5th.

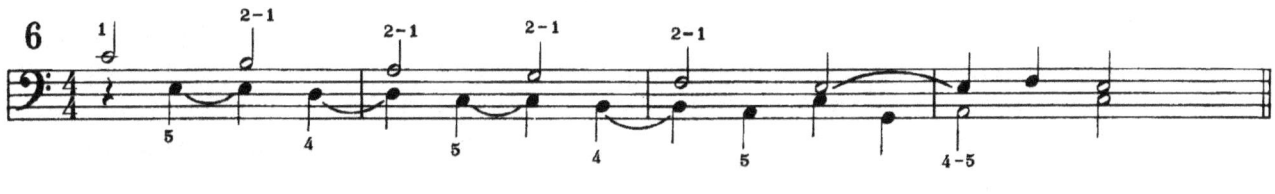

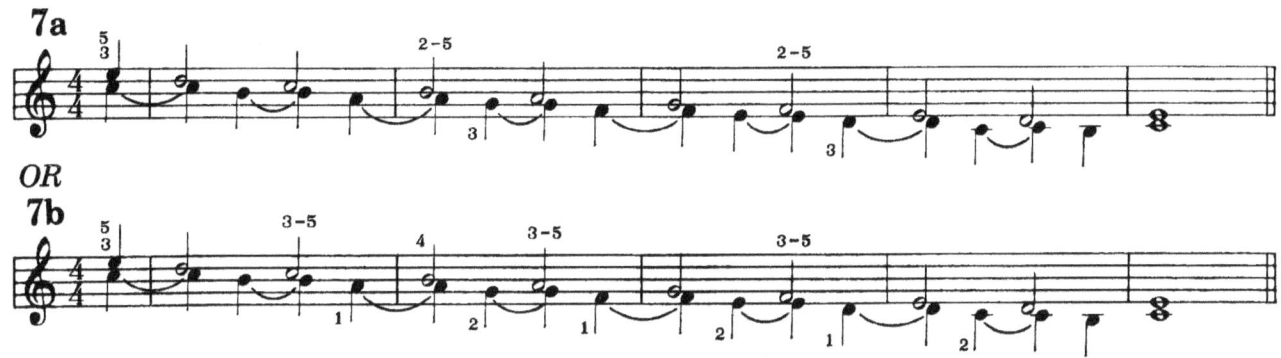

Note the 3rd finger crossing over the 5th.

Play separate hands and hands together.

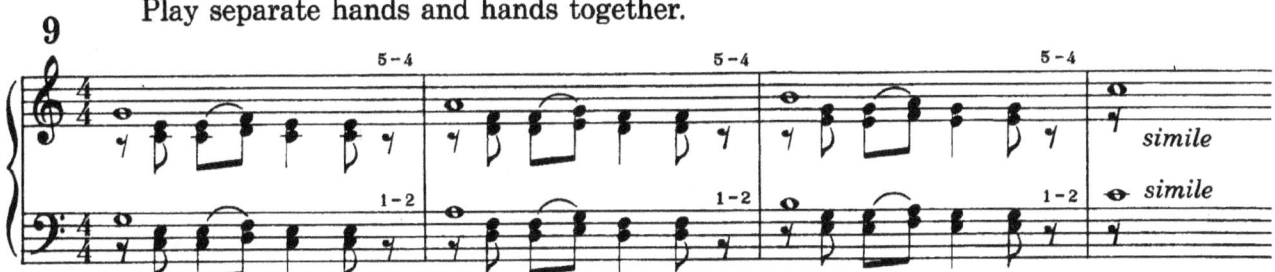

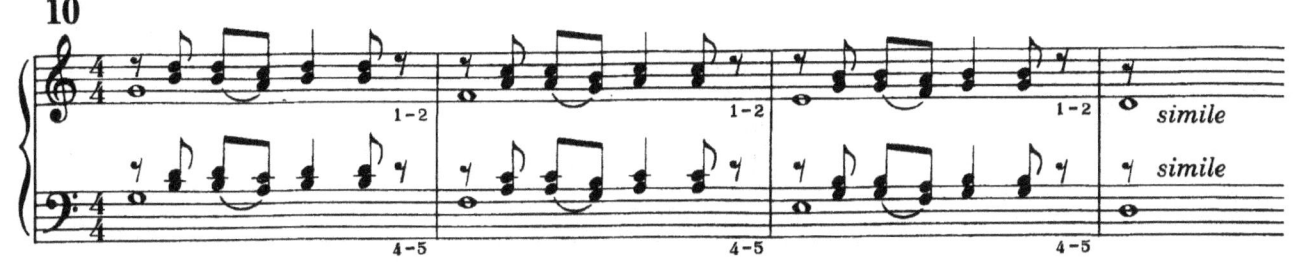

In numbers 9 and 10, execute the finger change on the last quaver count in each bar.

C AND F MELODIC MINOR SCALES

C MELODIC MINOR

The next two Melodic Minors, (C min and F min), are also a set. After playing C Minor Natural form (3 Flats — B, E, A, Relative to E Flat Major) raise the 6th and 7th degrees to A Natural and B Natural ascending and lower them to B Flat and A Flat in the descending form.

F MELODIC MINOR

The same goes for F Minor (4 Flats — B, E, A, D, Relative to A Flat Major). Raise the 6th and 7th degrees to D and E Naturals, ascending, and lower them to E and D Flats in the descending form. Make special note of the endings of these two scales: in the ascending form 6, 7 and 8 are all white notes and in the descending form 8 is white and both 7 and 6 are black.

Add these scales to those you are already practising on a rotation system. Remember that the fingering for each of the above scales is the same as for their respective Majors (F and C).

34. SARABANDE

This piece uses some of the part-playing techniques introduced on the previous pages. In this style of music the 4th and 5th fingers often cross over each other, to maintain the legato line. (L.H. Bars 4-5).

Note also the use of the thumb on a black note in the Right Hand in bars 8 and 9. This fingering is permissible in music written in a chordal style.

Mark the Modulations

CHORD TABLES

34. SARABANDE
(from Suite on the Chorale "Auf meinen lieben Gott")

DIETRICH BUXTEHUDE, 1637–1707
Danish, Early Baroque

MAJOR 6THS — Continued

Given below are the remaining five Major 6th and Minor 7th chords. They are: F sharp, C sharp, A flat, E flat and B flat Major 6ths and their corresponding minor 7th chords: E flat, B flat, F, C and G. (See page 131 for the theory behind them).

Play them in all inversions. Remember that the 3rd inversion of a Major 6th is in fact the corresponding Minor 7th.

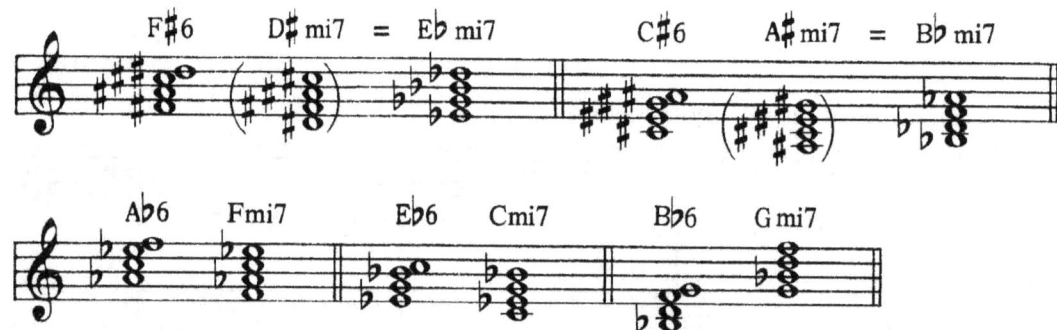

For further experience in Rock Piano patterns refer to the book 'Rock Piano Styles' by Matt Dennis. (Mel Bay Publications, available through Castle Music Australia).

CHORD PATTERN

Here is another Rock Pattern using the types of chords learnt up to now.

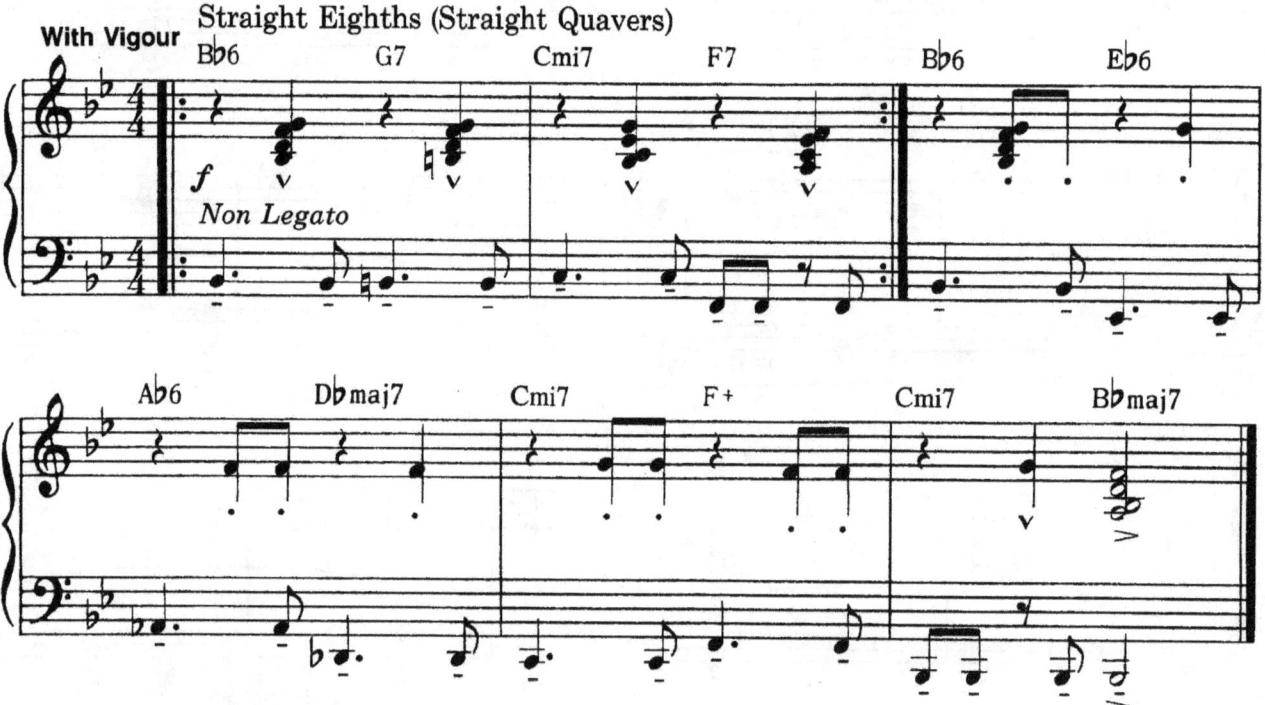

This is the same Rock Pattern arranged for Left Hand only. Play your own improvised melody in the Right Hand.

B FLAT, E FLAT AND A FLAT MELODIC MINOR SCALES

To those Melodic Minor scales already learnt (F, C, G, D, A, E and B) add the scales of B Flat, E Flat and A Flat Melodic Minor.

B FLAT MELODIC MINOR SCALE

Play B♭ Minor (5 flats — B, E, A, D, G — Relative to D♭ Major) in the Natural Minor Form first. Note the fact that you only have to concern yourself with 2 White Notes, F and C. To convert the scale to the Melodic form, raise the 6th and 7th degrees in the ascending scale to G and A Naturals and lower them back to A♭ and G♭ in the descending form. The fingering is exactly the same as for the Harmonic Form: Right Hand: 2 1 2 3 1 2 3 4 and Left Hand: 2 1 3 2 1 4 3 2.

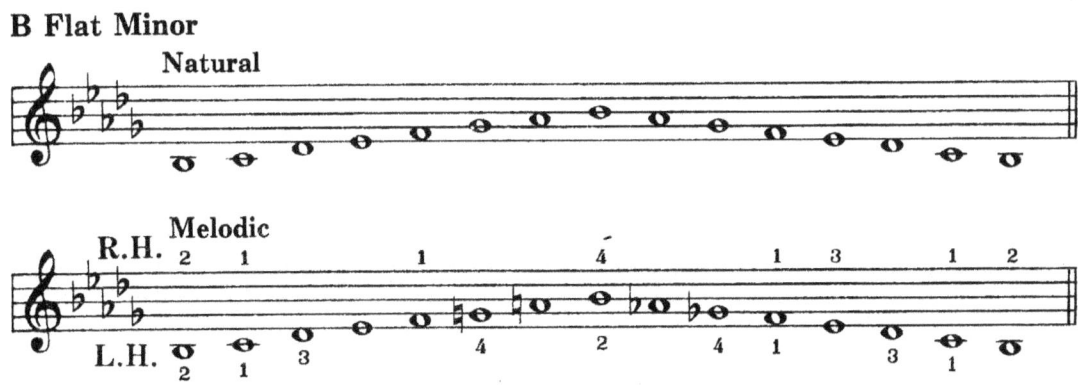

E FLAT MELODIC MINOR SCALE

Follow the same pattern for E♭ Minor (6 Flats — B, E, A, D, G, C — Relative to G♭ Major). Note that the only White notes are F and C♭ (B) in the Natural Form. Raise the 6th and 7th degrees in the ascending form to C and D Naturals and lower them to D♭ and C♭ in the descending form. The Right Hand fingering is 2 1 2 3 4 1 2 3 and the Left Hand fingering is 2 1 4 3 2 1 3 2. (Watch the Left Hand carefully).

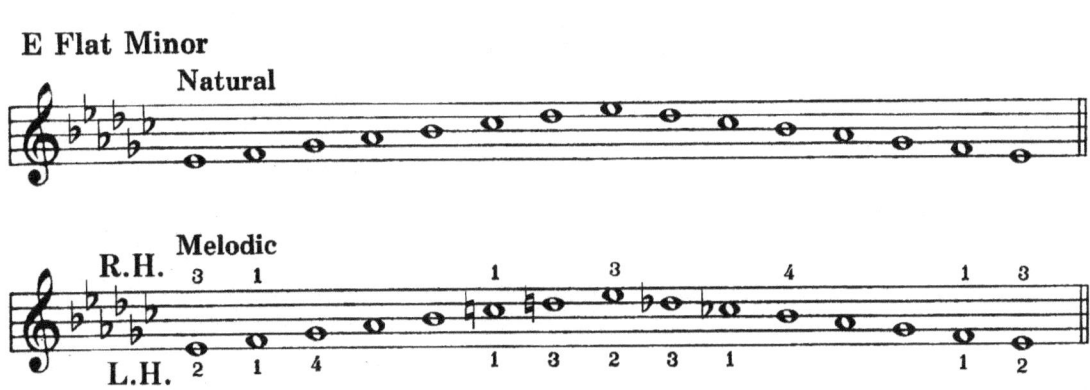

A FLAT MELODIC MINOR SCALE

A♭ Minor Natural form has 7 flats, B, E, A, D, G, C and F, Relative to C♭ Major. The only White notes in this form are C♭ and F♭, (B and E). In the ascending Melodic form the 6th and 7th degrees are raised to F and G Naturals and they are lowered back to F♭ and G♭ in the descending form. The Right Hand fingering for the scale is 3 4 1 2 3 1 2 3. The Left Hand fingering differs depending on the direction, i.e. in the ascending form it is:

Fingering: 3 2 1 4 3 2 1 3   and the descending form is: 3 2 1 3 2 1 4 3
Degree: 1 2 3 4 5 6 7 8   Degree: 1 2 3 4 5 6 7 8

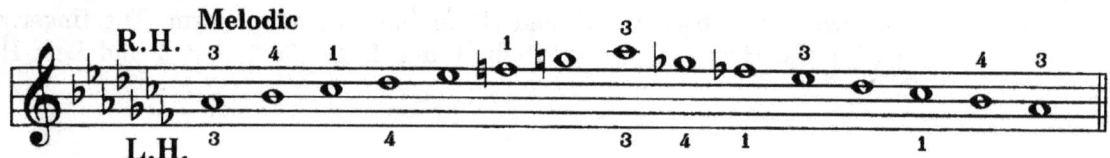

BASIC CHA CHA RHYTHMS:
Straight Eight

THE CHA-CHA-CHA

The Cha-Cha-Cha was developed in 1962 in the United States. The dance is a derivative of the Mambo which was too difficult a dance for the general public. The dance is still regarded as the most popular of the Latin-American dances.

35. CHACABUCO CHA CHA CHA

CHORD TABLES

CHACABUCO CHA CHA CHA

Clap the timing on each separate stave before playing this piece.

MINOR SIXTH AND MINOR SEVENTH FLATTENED FIFTH CHORDS

To build a Minor 6th chord simply take a Major 6th chord and lower the third degree by a semitone. (The minor part refers only to the triad). In classical terminology this chord would be known as a minor triad with an added 6th.

The Minor 6th chord is found on the second degree of the major scale. For instance in C Major the second degree is D and the sixth chord built up on this note becomes D, F, A and B. Thus you will find that a Minor 6th chord occurs more frequently in a Major key on the second degree than as the Tonic chord of a Minor key.

When the inversions are worked out on this chord you will find that the third inversion is another chord in its own right. This chord which would be B, D, F and A in the case of D mi6 inverted, is known as the B "Minor 7th, Flattened 5th" (mi7 ♭5) or as the "Half Diminished 7th" chord.

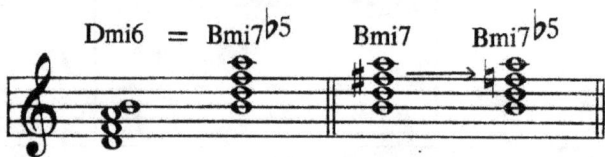

(Remember that B diminished 7th would be B, D, F and A♭ whereas B half-diminished consists of a diminished triad (B, D and F) plus a minor seventh interval B to A). The symbol for a half-diminished 7th chord is a circle with a line through it, thus ∅. Both of these names for this chord are in common usage although in club charts it is recommended that the half-diminished sign be avoided.

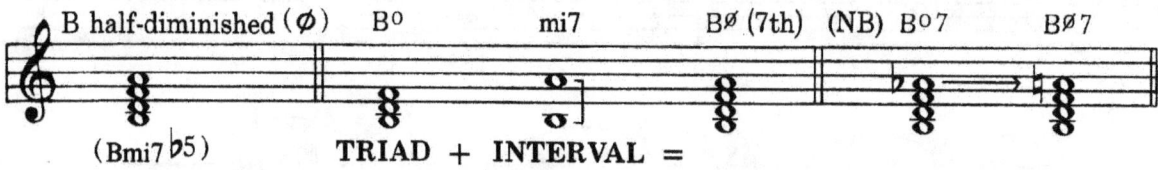

The half-diminished seventh chord (min7 flat 5) is found on the seventh degree of the Major scale. It is a leading function chord and has therefore a strong pull to resolve onto the Tonic Chord.

It is also found as the Seventh chord built on the Second degree of the Harmonic and Natural Minor scales. A common progression of chords in a Minor Key is from the second degree (ii7 — Half-Dim 7th) to the Fifth degree (V7 — Dom 7th) to the Tonic Chord (i).

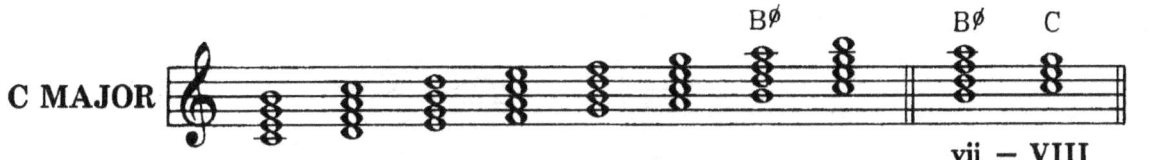

Learn the Minor 6th chords and their corresponding half-diminished (mi7♭5) chords on the following notes:

Mi6 on — F, C, G, D, A, E, B and Mi7♭5 on D, A, E, B, F sharp, C sharp and G sharp.

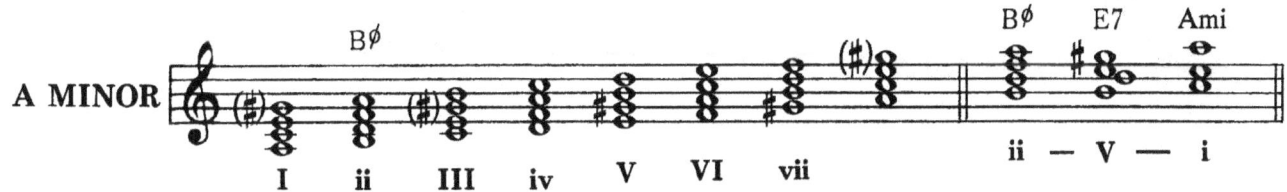

Practise all chords and inversions in the form given on page 53.

THE RUMBA

The Rumba originated in the southern section of Cuba which was mainly populated by Negroes. Cuban music is a mixture of Spanish and African popularly known as Afro-Cuban. The Spanish Rhythm is usually a combination of 6/8 and 3/4 and the Afro-Cuban Rhythm from that area is based on the figure:

The Rumba is regarded as one of the Amorous dances in which the partners hold each other closely. (The others are the Tango and the Merengue).

The Rumba rhythm in this tune is based on the Cuban Cinquillo (5 notes)

which results in performance of the basic rhythm given above. The Cinquillo is usually further shortened to

36. JUCARO RUMBA

CHORD TABLES

JUCARO RUMBA

M.M. ♩ = 90–126

MELODIC MINOR SCALES   (Last instalment)

The last two Melodic Minor scales to learn are F sharp and C sharp Melodics. They both have a special fingering in the right hand.

F SHARP MELODIC MINOR

F sharp Melodic is related to A Major (3 sharps — F, C and G). After playing the Natural Minor form, raise the 6th and 7th degrees to D sharp and E sharp (F white note) on the way up, and lower them to E natural and D natural on the way back. Play the left hand first, with this fingering: 4 3 2 1 3 2 1 3. The right hand fingering for both this scale and C sharp Melodic has two forms, one for the ascending scale and one for the descending scale.

The ascending scale is: 2 3 1 2 3 4 1 3   and descending is: 3 4 1 2 3 1 2 3
         Degree: 1 2 3 4 5 6 7 8   Degree: 1 2 3 4 5 6 7 8

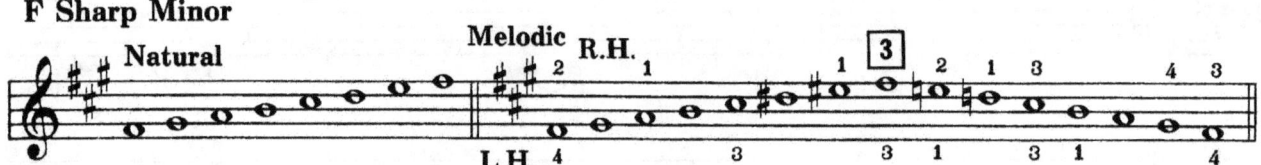

C SHARP MELODIC MINOR

C sharp Melodic is related to E Major (4 sharps F, C, G and D). After playing the Natural Minor form, raise the 6th and 7th degrees to A♯ and B♯ (C white note) in the ascending form. The right hand fingering is as above, and the left hand fingering is the same as for C sharp Major (i.e. 3 2 1 4 3 2 1 3). Add these scales to the other Melodics previously learnt and play them in a rotation system like that suggested on page 129.

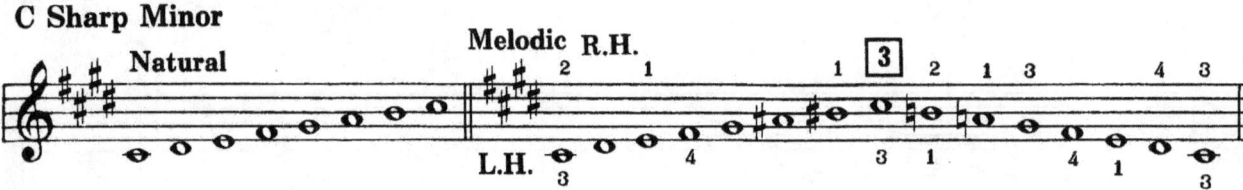

CYCLE OF FIFTHS

Here is the full cycle including Major Keys and their relative Minor keys (in the inner circle).

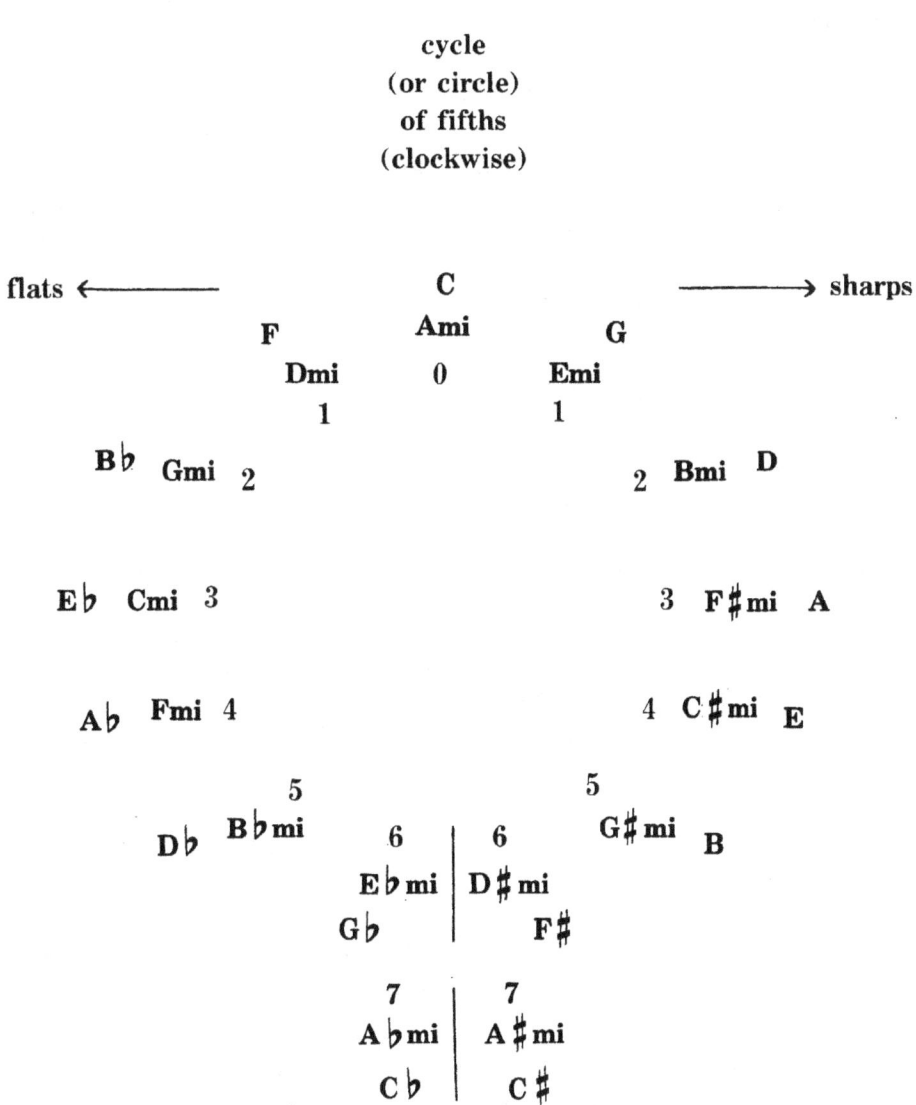

MAJOR SCALES — 2 OCTAVES

At this stage you should add the scales that begin on the black notes, B flat, E flat, A flat, D flat and F sharp, to those that are already being practised over a two-octave range. They are in fact easier than the white-note forms as the scale simply repeats itself without any change to the fingering. Just keep in mind where the 4th finger goes and the rest of the scale will take care of itself.

THE BOSSA NOVA (The New Beat)

The credit for the popularisation of this distinctive Brazilian rhythm is attributed to the Brazilian composer Antonio Carlos Jobim. In the 1960's the Bossa Nova rhythm became widely known through many of Jobim's songs, for example "The Girl from Ipanema", "Desafinado", "Meditation", "Wave" and "Quiet Nights of Quiet Stars" to name a few.

The rhythm itself was not taken up popularly by dancers and therefore is now more often used in the "Dinner Music" and quiet listening repertoire.

A feature of the rhythm is that it is symmetrical and can be read in mirror image, forwards or backwards. It is a two-bar rhythm which can be seen as a further development of the Rumba.

The Bossa Nova rhythm is [musical notation in 4/4]

Note that the number of quavers in each unit is either 3 or 4. Thus the rhythm could be read 3, 3, 4, 3, 3.

The Bossa Nova rhythm has been adapted to suit Disco music in the late 1970's and early 1980's. In some cases it is still written over two bars, as in "I go to Rio" by Peter Allen. However, in the majority of cases it has had all the time values reduced by half, and is written over one bar.

Thus: [musical notation in 4/4]

Owing to the Latin flavour of the Disco repertoire, much of the music of the earlier decades of this century has been revived with a Disco flavour and is acceptable to both young and old.

Improvisation over a Chord Pattern

When improvising over a series of chords belonging to one key, a good way to achieve an interesting sound which blends well with the chords, is to play the scale of the home key over the range from the **first degree to the ninth degree,** both ascending and descending. If the melody is in common time and you play the scale is in either straight or swing eighth notes, then generally you will find that the degrees which blend with the chords fall on the strong beats. Experiment with the **I vi ii V I** progression to hear how this works.

If a tune modulates, use the 'Spider Chart' to find the keys and change your scale to suit the sections of the piece, continuing to run it from 1 to 9 and back. Apply this system to the completed chord chart on page 159.

37. BOSSA NOVA DE BONDI

In this piece, several functional pianistic styles are demonstrated. The Introduction and Coda sections demonstrate the style of playing, which would be employed when the pianist was acting as an accompanist to a Front Line instrument, such as Trumpet or Flute, or accompanying a vocalist. The left Hand is providing the Bass Line and the Right Hand is providing the chords.

If a Bass player were present to take over the Bass Line, the pianist could either
(1) omit the Bass line altogether, while playing fuller versions of the chords split between the two hands, or
(2) play the Bass line very softly so as not to interfere with the Bass player (or cause a clash of tuning — sometimes pianos are not exactly in tune and it is hard for the Bass player to match the tuning of the piano).

In sections A and B of the piece, the style demonstrated is the one used when the pianist is required to supply both the Melody and Chords. In a band situation, the Bass player would provide the Root Notes of the chords in the lower register, playing a line very similar to the Bass line in the Introduction.

Section C demonstrates that when the melody moves into the Middle register of the keyboard (or lower) the Left Hand accompaniment should be thinned out so as not to override the melody. (Note the open 5ths, 6ths and 7ths.)

COLOUR AND CLAP

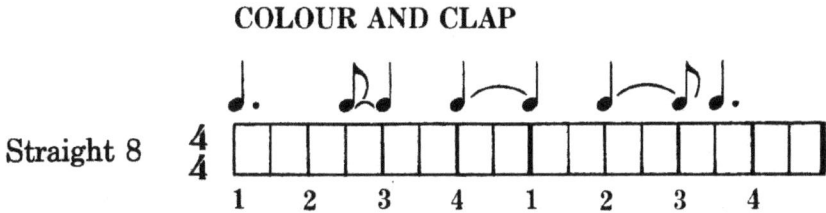

CHORD TABLES

Write the Chord names above each bar.

BOSSA NOVA DE BONDI

M.M. ♩ = 120–126

159

Write out the chord symbols from the Bossa Nova de Bondi, then play them in the Left Hand, either as held chords or as four chords per bar or in the Bossa Nova rhythm.

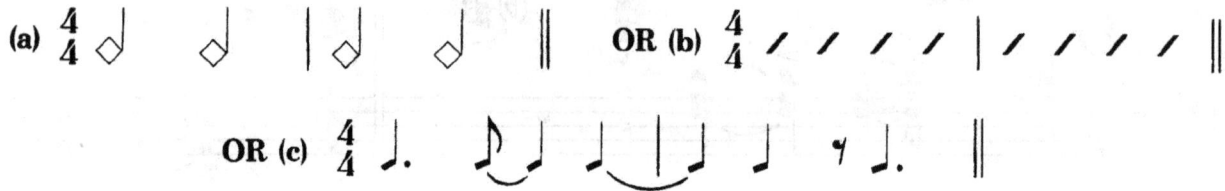

Improvise a Right-Hand melody over the chords.

PLAYING MUSIC WITH A SWING FEEL

The description 'swing' is used for most music interpreted with a triplet feel. The manner in which it is written can vary. The ways swing music can be written were discussed on page 80 in Book 2A. The swing feel is sometimes even written as 12/8.

This style of music developed in America in the 1940s and was an off shoot of the earlier Boogie and Blues styles The chief instrumental exponents of the style were Benny Goodman, Glenn Miller, Jimmy Lunceford, Count Basie and their big bands.

Many song stylists sang in the swing style, particularly Frank Sinatra, Sarah Vaughan, Tony Bennet, Joe Williams, Ella Fitzgerald, Mel Torme, and more recently Harry Connick Jnr has carried the tradition forward.

To see the various ways swing style can be written, refer to the Blues and Boogie-Woogie (Brandman) where the first five pieces are all written with a different figure, but are interpreted the same way, that is with the first eighth note being given two thirds the length of a quarter note, and the second eighth, the remaining third. See the indication over this Swing example. In Swing music the accents fall on the second and fourth beats of the bar in Common Time and the last third of the beat, that is the second of two eighth notes, is given emphasis.

This eight bar chord pattern in swing style, uses some of the common comping figures found in swing tunes. To comp means to fill in with rhythmic punctuations and syncopation.&; The last two bars are written with the Count Basie trademark rhythmic pattern.

Refer also to the rhythmic punctuation in Kerin Bailey's piece Al's Cafe on the following pages and to his tune Count Basics in Book 2 of the Jazzin' Around Series.

SWINGIN' IN STYLE

Al's Café

This piece in swing style is by Australian composer Kerin Bailey. Kerin is a respected composer and jazz pianist who has composed a series of piano pieces available in five books in the *Jazzin' Around* series. They also have accompanying backing tracks on SMF discs or the *Jazzin' Around Plus* CD. Other works for piano include *Six Sketches* and *Triplet Falls*. Many of his pieces have been nominated as examination list pieces.

Al's Cafe typifies many of the swing sounds and rhythms. It is composed in 8 bar sections AABA followed by a written out improvisation and then a return to the B section and a final Coda. Bailey uses many harmonic devices to create the jazzy sound.

Activities

1. Write the Modulation points for this piece

2. Write a chord table and extend each of the chords to the seventh.
   (Refer to the Contemporary Chord Workbook for more information.)

3. Find the harmonic devices used in this tune.

   a) Pedal Point (hint: look at bars 1-5) . Find any other instances of Pedal Point in this tune. (Refer to Book 2A of this course for information on Pedal Point.)

   b) Cycle of Fifth progressions. Find the **I vi ii V I** progression in line 4 and the longer cycle progression in the coda Indicate this with the cycle logo (bicycle)

   c) Locate the Minor 7 flat 5 chords in this piece and circle them in red.

   d) locate the other altered chord, the Dom7 flat 5 chord. What is its letter name? ......

   e) Find the extended chords 9ths and 13ths and listen to their sound. More information on all these chords can be found in Book 3 of this course, or Books 1 and 2 of the Contemporary Chord Workbook series.

4. Once you have learnt the piece, improvise your own melody over the chord progression.

38. AL'S CAFÉ

Kerin Bailey

Medium fast swing ♩ = 176

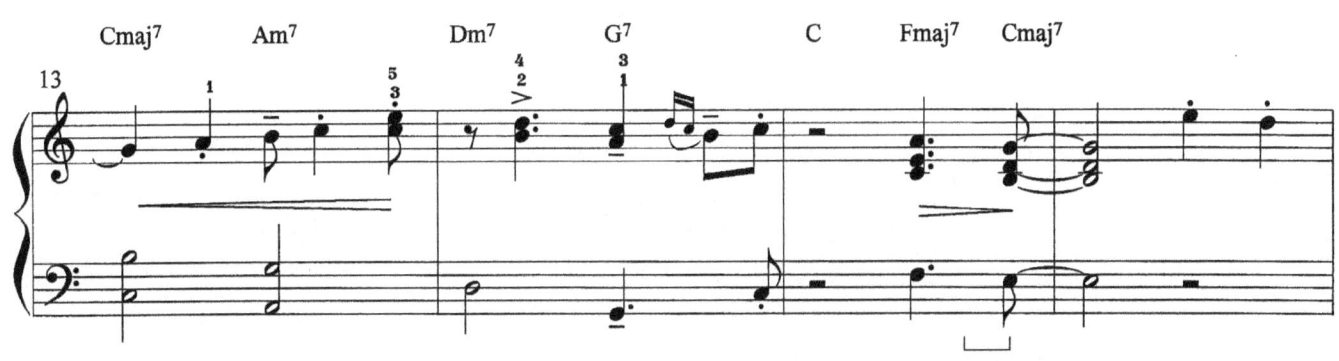

© 1994 Kerin Bailey Music. Used by kind permission.

THE 12/8 BALLAD

Many songs which are basically written in 4/4 and are of slow tempo can be treated as a 12/8 ballad. Usually the pianist is required to play either arpeggio figures or block chord figures on every pulse. The Time Signature is usually marked 12/8 to avoid having to write the triplet sign over every beat, however, sometimes the triplets are marked and the time signature is left as 4/4. One example of this type of tune is the song "Can't Help Falling in Love" recorded by Elvis Presley.

39. BLUEBERRY BALLAD

Write the Chord names above each bar.

MORE MINOR SIXTH AND MINOR SEVENTH FLATTENED FIFTH CHORDS

Final Minor Sixth Chords. Add the last 5 minor sixth chords and their corresponding half — diminished sevenths (Min 7 flattened 5th), to those previously learnt. They are F sharp, C sharp, A flat, E flat and B flat Minor 6ths and correspondingly: E flat, B flat, F, C and G half-diminished 7th chords.

Practise all minor sixth chords in inversions (both block and broken) in the form given on page 53.

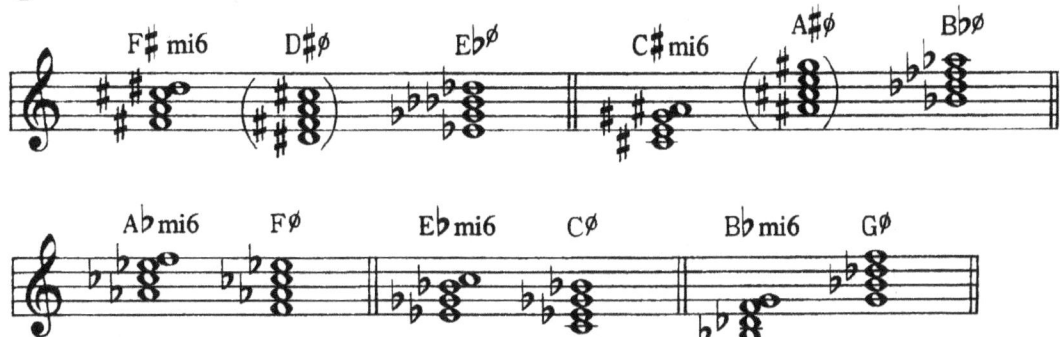

40. BENEATH THE COOLABAH TREE

This piece uses some 'add 9' chords and the half-diminished 7th chord. Refer to CPM book 3

ADAGIO - (Ital. = *ad agio,* "at ease" "leisurely")

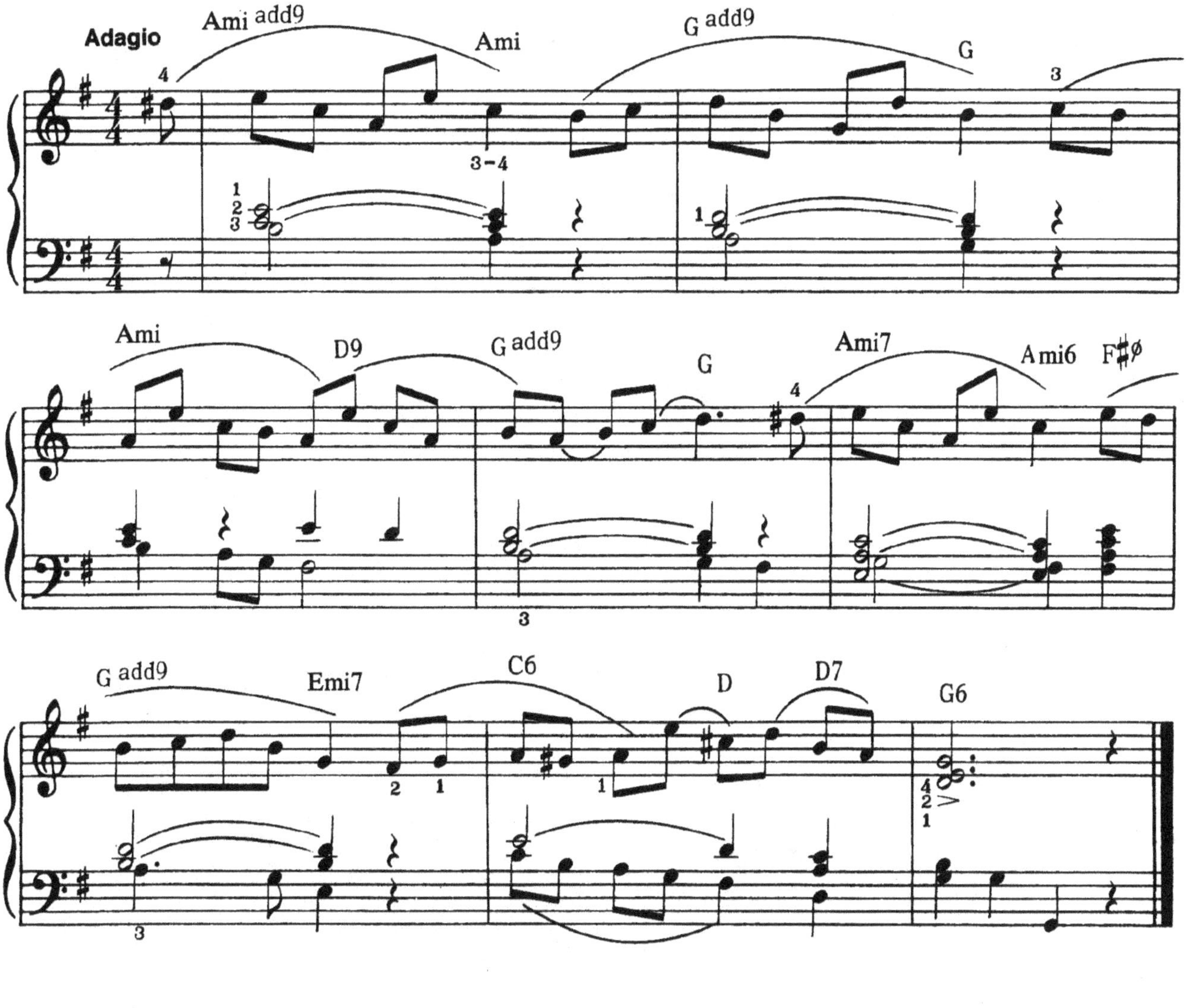

CROTCHET TRIPLETS

In Book 1, Quaver Triplets were introduced: a Triplet of three quavers is played in the time of 2 ordinary quavers, total value 1 crotchet.

Thus: ♪♪♪ = ♪♪ = ♩

The same principle applies to CROTCHET TRIPLETS. Three Crotchets, under a Triplet Bracket, are played in the time of two ordinary crotchets, total value 1 minim.

Thus: ♩♩♩ = ♩♩ = 𝅗𝅥

The Bracket usually used over the Crotchet Triplet is a square bracket.

The Crotchet Triplet most often occurs in a Simple Time Signature, where the bar can be divided into minims (half-notes). For example 2/4, 4/4 or 2/2, 3/2 or 4/2 time.

There are 2 ways to count a Crotchet Triplet:

1. If possible count the previous bars in terms of a minim (half-note) beat (𝅗𝅥) so that the Beat can be divided into 2, 3 or 4 parts. If playing in 4/4 for instance, change the counting to that of 2/2 shortly before the Crotchet Triplet occurs and then change back to 4/4 counting when it has been played. For example:

2. If the Crotchet Triplet has to be superimposed over two crotchet beats (played against two crotchet beats) find the common denominator between the two types of time values and count the section in terms of this.

In this case the common denominator is that both the 2 crotchets and the crotchet triplet could be subdivided into a set of 6 quavers. (Both 2 and 3 divide into 6).

The 2 crotchets can be subdivided into quaver triplets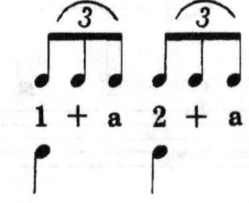

and each of the Crotchet Triplet notes can be given two of these quaver counts. Thus:

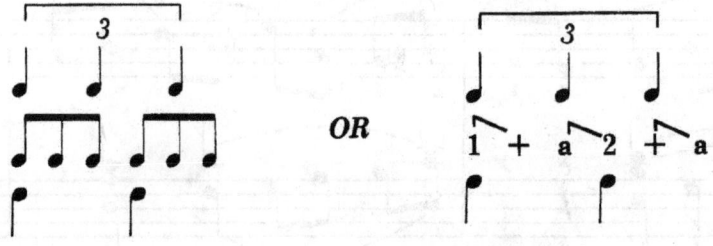

Practise clapping this unit taking the Crotchet Triplet in one hand and the two crotchets in the other. When combining them, note that they fall on the **1+a 2+a**. When playing crotchet triplets in swing timing they will be easy to feel as everything else is counted in Quaver Triplets.

For example:

THE DUPLET

The word Duplet comes from the latin "duplus" meaning "two". Whereas a Triplet is **three** notes played in the time of **two** of the same value, a DUPLET is a group of **two** notes played in the time of **three** of the same value.

Duplets occur only in Compound Time Signatures where the Beat Note normally divides into three parts. Thus in 6/4, the dotted minim (𝅗𝅥.) beat which usually would subdivide into three crotchets could be divided into two crotchets using a Crotchet Duplet.

Likewise in 6/8 the dotted crotchet beat note could be subdivided into two parts by using a Quaver Duplet.

The method of counting a Duplet is the reverse of counting the Triplet.

1. If possible try to count the previous bars in terms of the Duplet: i.e. divide each beat into 2 parts and count 1 + 2 +   instead of   1 2 3 4 5 6

2. If the Crotchet Duplet has to be superimposed (played against) three crotchets in 6/4 time for instance, once again find the common denominator between the two units (6). Continue counting the 3 crotchet beats 1 + 2 + 3 + and bring the duplet in on the 1st count and on the half way point. Thus:

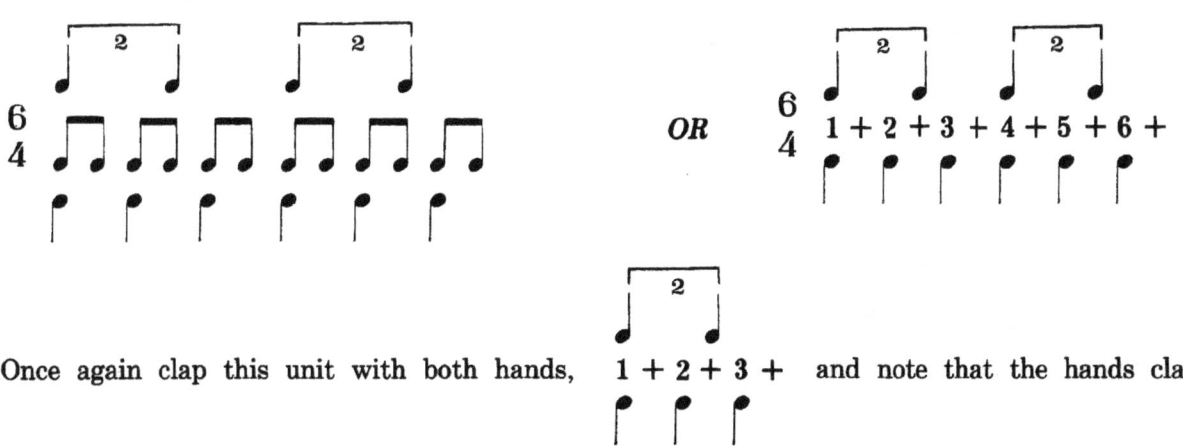

Once again clap this unit with both hands,   1 + 2 + 3 +   and note that the hands clap on <u>1</u> + <u>2</u> + <u>3</u> + , and that it sounds exactly the same as the Triplet played against 2 beats.

41. SPIDERSWING

Key and Modulations

1) What is the key of this piece? Remember to look at the key signature and the final chord ....

2) Fill in the modulation points for this piece. Place the number of flats in the boxes and the key centres (tonics of the keys) in the circles.

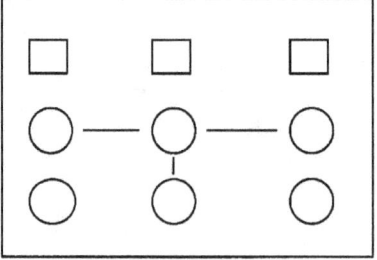

3) This piece travels to every key in the modulation point diagram you have completed. Rewrite the modulation points in the centre and complete the 'legs' (that is: the chord tables) for each of the keys in the **'Spider'** on the facing page.

4) Each key lasts for approximately four bars. Find the keys used for each four-bar section of the piece and indicate them over the music using a bracket.

5) Analyse the chords and the progressions used.

6) Look for any use of the Cycle progressions and mark them with a bracket and with the cycle symbol.

7) Indicate the cadences at the end of each four-bar section.

Form

The piece is in four sections **A B C A** (repeated) plus a short coda.
Note the use of the walking bass line and the 'comping' figures in the B section.

Style

The piece is to be played at a moderate tempo using the swing feel.

Pairs of eighth notes are interpreted with triplet feel.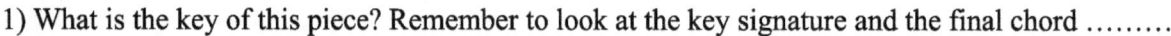

To achieve the swing feel, place the emphasis on the final third of the beat.

This figure   is interpreted

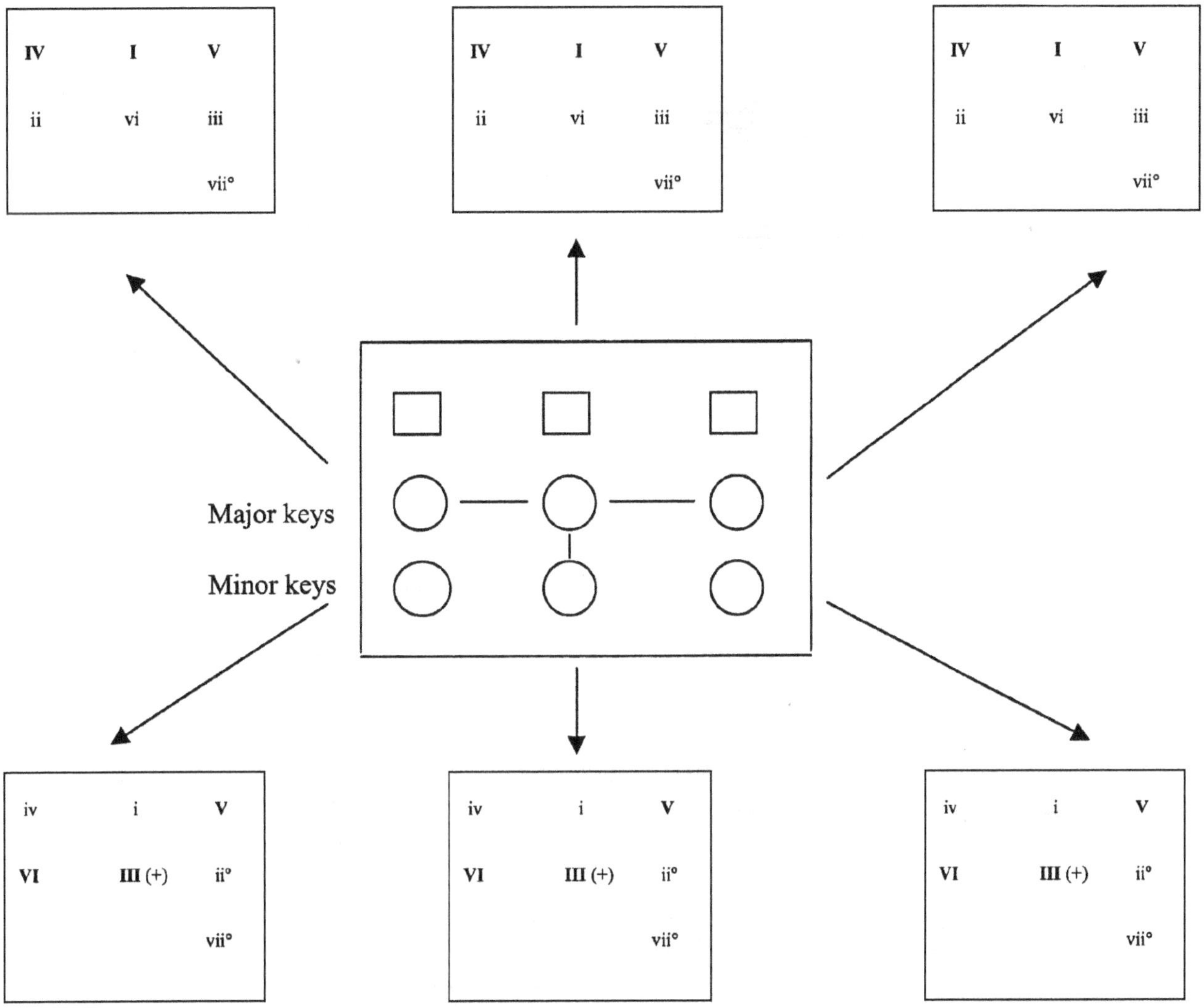

MODULATION SPIDER

170

IV	I	V
ii	vi	iii
		vii°

IV	I	V
ii	vi	iii
		vii°

IV	I	V
ii	vi	iii
		vii°

Major keys

Minor keys

iv	i	V
VI	III (+)	ii°
		vii°

iv	i	V
VI	III (+)	ii°
		vii°

iv	i	V
VI	III (+)	ii°
		vii°

41. SPIDERSWING

Margaret Brandman

Moderate swing tempo

*Dom7 flat 9
see Contemporary Chord Workbook 2

RHYTHMIC CHORD PATTERNS

The following chord patterns are written in some more of the Latin-American rhythms and contemporary accompaniment styles.

THE CONGA

The Conga is one of the Carnival dances of Afro-Cuban origin. The dance is performed during "Compassas" or parades and its rhythm is essentially a march except for the anticipation. It is a popular dance at parties where the dancers form a Conga Line with each person placing his hands on the waist of the person in front.

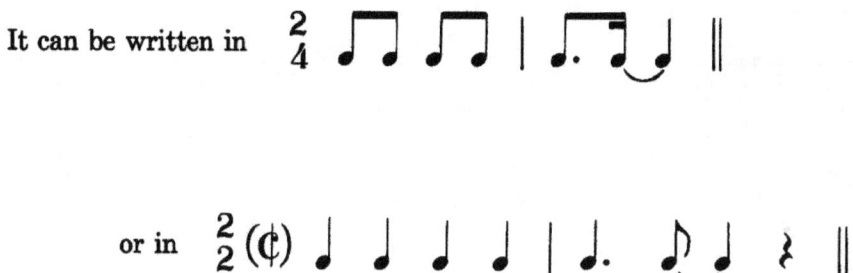

M.M. ♩ = 112   Write the Chord names above the bars.

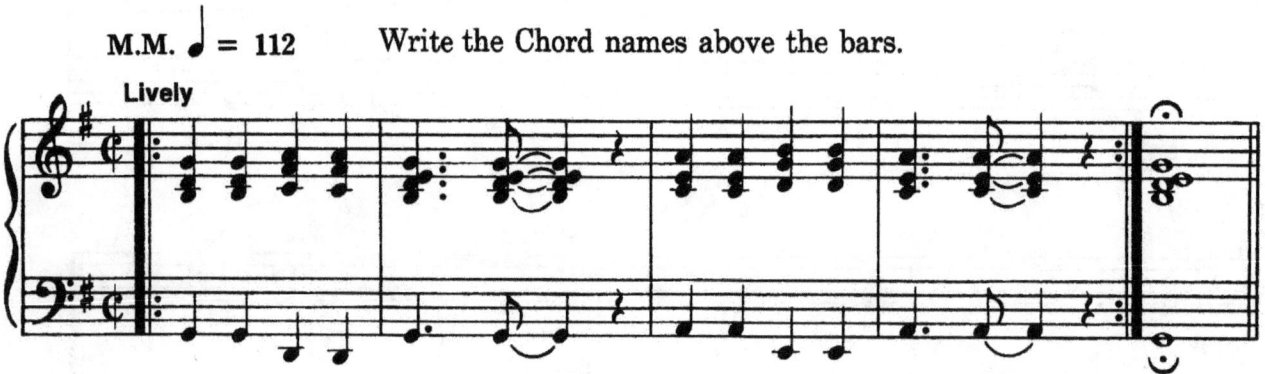

MOTOWN

The word Motown comes from the shortening of two words — Motor Town. In the United States the city of Detroit is the main motor vehicle manufacturing centre, and it is from this town that the Motown musicians came.

The Motown record label was formed by Berry Gordy jnr. The musicians who recorded under this label and influenced the sound were mainly black musicians, notably Stevie Wonder, The Supremes with Diana Ross, The Four Tops, Smokey Robinson and Marvin Gaye.

✷ Short-Hand chords. See explanation on page 181.

42. JINGLE BELLS - Disco/Reggae arrangement

The arrangement of the following piece uses 'add 9' chords (see CPM Bk 3) and two different styles of rhythmic accompaniment. See pages 175 (verse) & 176 (chorus)
VERSE : The verse is accompanied by a 'Disco' figure in the Left Hand in the middle register of the instrument, while the melody is played an octave higher.
CHORUS : The Chorus (main tune) has been arranged with a bass line which suggests a reggae feel.

Reggae is a style of rhythmic accompaniment which emerged from Jamaica in the 1960s and was made famous by 'Bob Marley and the Wailers.' The Reggae rhythm is distinguished by the syncopated bass lines, which often drop out on the first beat, or leave long rests, which encourages the listener to move in order to fill the gap. This makes listeners feel like dancing! . The eighth notes are treated with a shuffle or swing feel.

Clap and play the following Reggae rhythms.

42. JINGLE BELLS

J. Pierpoint

Arrangement by Margaret S. Brandman.

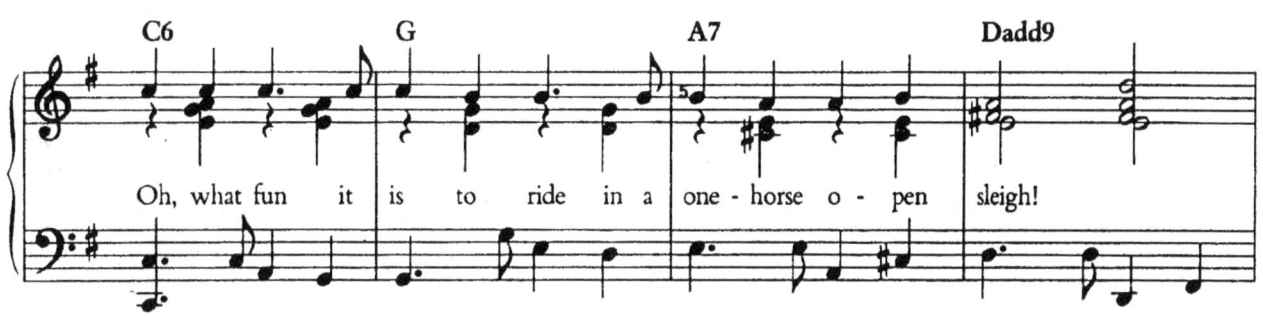

*For more exciting and unusual arrangements of Christmas songs, refer to **Christmas Favourites** (Brandman)*

THE BEGUINE

The Beguine comes from the French islands of St Lucia and Martinique in the West Indies. The word "béguin" means "flirtation". The rhythm was made famous by the tune "Begin the Beguine" by Cole Porter.

BASIC BEGUINE RHYTHM:

40. BENNY'S BEGUINE

COLOUR AND CLAP

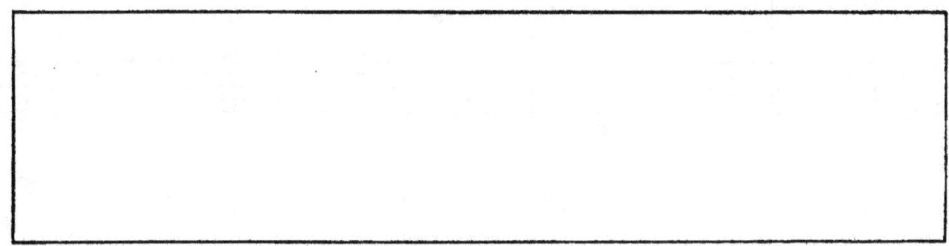

Straight 8

CHORD TABLES

Write the Chord names above each bar.

M.M. ♩ = 100

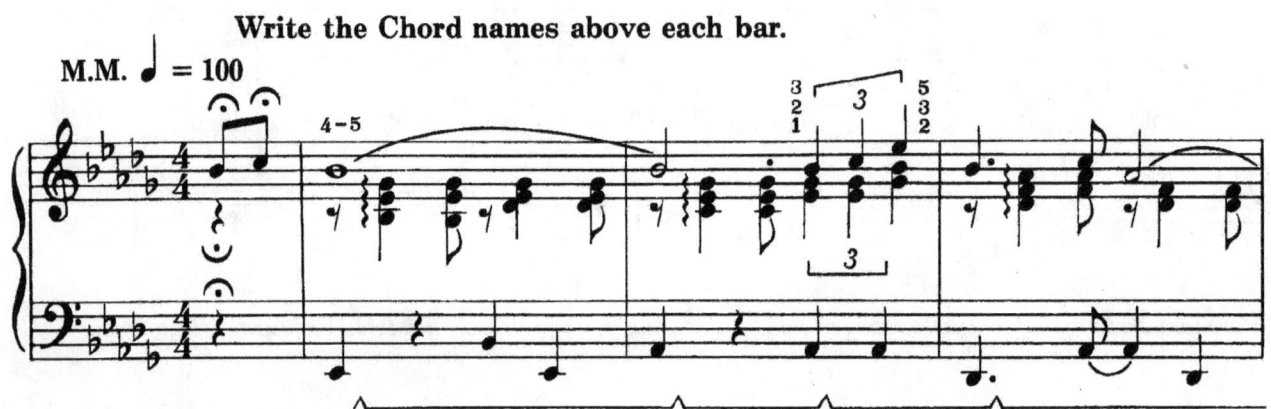

JAZZ-ROCK, FUNK AND DISCO FIGURES

The following patterns contain some contemporary figures that are frequently found in piano arrangements.

This first figure derives from the Bossa Nova rhythm demonstrated in Bossa Nova de Bondi (p156) It is the same rhythm played double time. It was a popular rhythm in tunes in the 1970s and 1980s.

Something Extra
Locate a copy of *I go to Rio* by Australian singer-songwriter Peter Allen, to play an extended section of this rhythm.

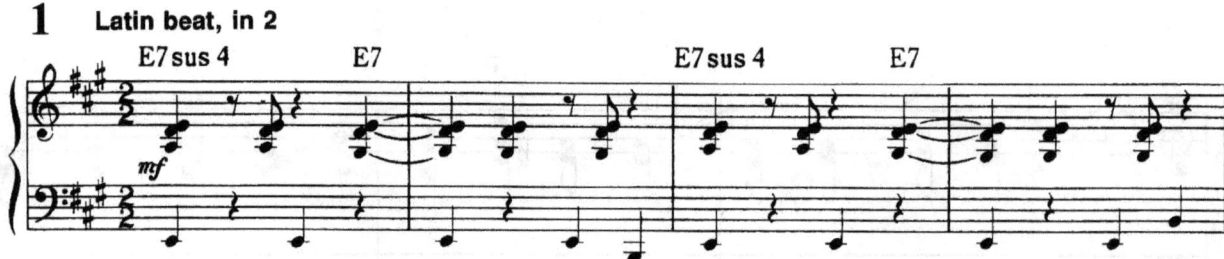

Here is the same rhythm written in rhythmic diminution. Every note value is halved so that the entire rhythm fits in one bar.

This figure reverses the rhythm in the two halves of the bar.

180

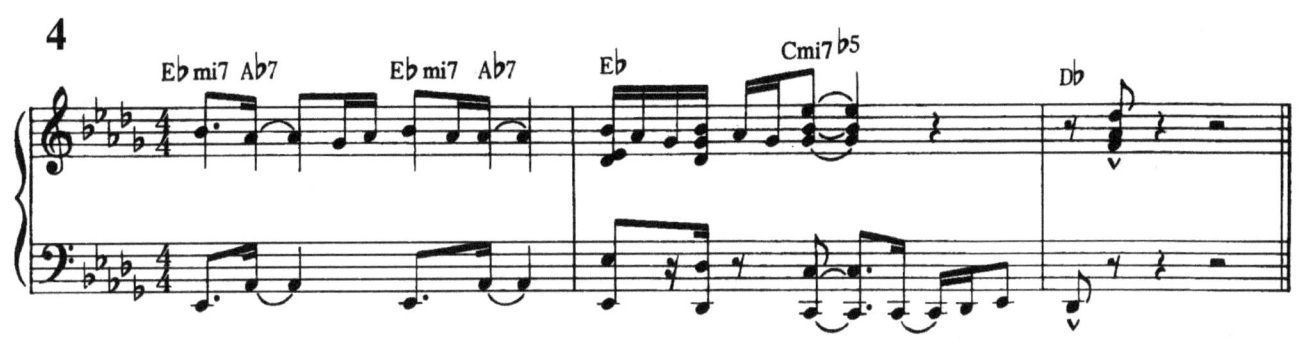

44. FUNKY DANCIN'

Many of the chords in this piece are written in the short-hand style, where only the top note is given and the player is required to supply the remainder. These short-hand chords are distinguished by stems which extend beyond the note-heads.

e.g.

Thus all the chord patterns in this piece employ two or more notes even if only the top note is written.

Ensure that the Melody line is kept separate from the accompaniment, by playing the inner parts "Mezzo-Piano" and with a light touch.

Clap the timing through before playing this piece.

CHORD TABLES

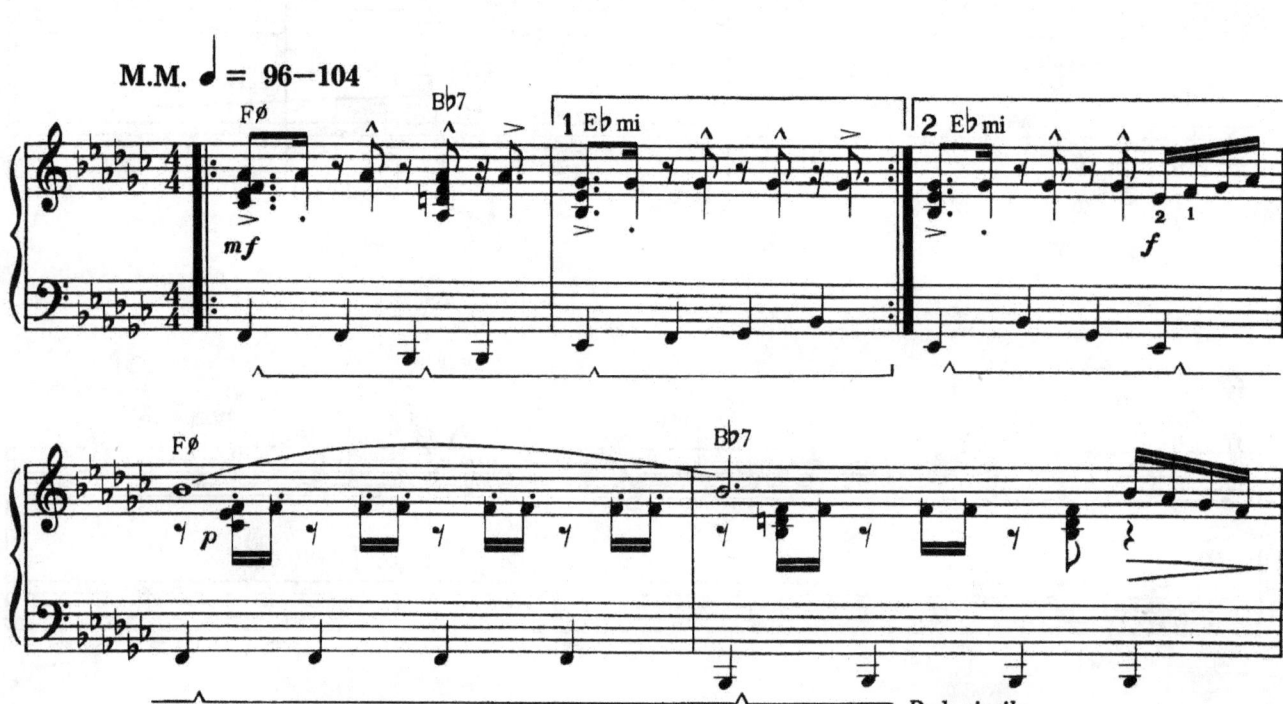

SIMPLE AND COMPOUND INTERVALS

Simple Intervals

Up to this stage we have talked about intervals up to an Octave. (8th). These intervals — Unison, 2nd, 3rd, 4th, 5th, 6th, 7th and 8th are all known as "Simple" Intervals.

Compound Intervals

Intervals of larger numerical value are known as "Compound" Intervals. They are the intervals of a 9th, 10th, 11th, 12th, 13th, 14th and 15th.

The names of the notes in an interval of a 9th are the same as those in the interval of a 2nd the only difference being that the 9th is an octave further away than a 2nd.

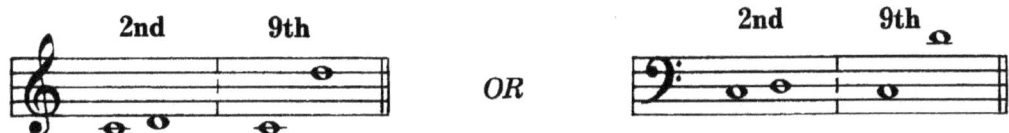

Similarly, the names of the notes in the interval of a 10th are the same as those in the interval of a 3rd; the 11th and the 4th, the 12th and the 5th, and so on.

Thus the larger intervals can be named 2 ways:

1. as a 9th	OR	2. as a Compound 2nd
as a 10th		as a Compound 3rd
as a 11th		as a Compound 4th
as a 12th		as a Compound 5th
as a 13th		as a Compound 6th
as a 14th		as a Compound 7th
as a 15th		as a Compound 8th

The interval qualities remain the same for both the Simple and Compound Intervals.

The Perfect Intervals are: both the Simple and Compound 1, 4, 5, 8
(11, 12, 15).

The Consonant Intervals are: both the Simple and Compound 3 and 6
(10 and 13).

The Dissonant Intervals are: both the Simple and Compound 2 and 7
(9 and 14).

Compound intervals are usually found between changes of position, for instance where the hand position moves up an octave plus a fifth (12th). In those cases use the Octave — Hopping technique (with finger swaps) and then feel the next distance (5th, 6th, etc.) from the 5-finger or Octave Hand Positions.

The other common place to find Compound intervals is when reading the distance between the two hands, for instance, if the Left Hand is playing C and the Right Hand is playing E

the distance between the two notes is a 10th (Compound 3rd).

The largest Hand-Span that is comfortable for most people is a 9th, (people with small hands can only reach an octave and those with quite large hands can sometimes reach a 10th with ease). As a result the player is usually not required to play Compound Intervals with one hand, although in more advanced pieces (usually written by piano players with large hand spans) 9ths and 10ths may be written and can be played "split" (one note after the other) if the hands cannot reach both notes at the same time.

THE SAMBA

The Samba is a Brazilian dance of Negro origin, (all the Brazilian and Cuban dances of Negro origin have two-syllable names, which are onomatopoeic suggesting the drum sounds, e.g. Conga, Lundu, Bamba, etc.).

The Samba is one of the Carnival Dances. The other is the Conga. The Basic Samba rhythm is often combined with the Tango, Rumba and Foxtrot rhythms to form hybrid versions of the dance. In Brazil, the forms of the Samba sung and danced in the country vary from those danced in the city.

The Samba-Cancao (Samba Song) is a type of nostalgic serenade which is quite different in character to the standard Samba. The song "Brazil" and the following tune are both examples of this type of Samba.

However, all forms of the Samba have three things in common, the Duple Meter, the Major Key and bright tempo.

45. SYDNEY SAMBA

CHORD TABLES

SYDNEY SAMBA

Be careful to bring out the melody line over the accompaniment.
Use a Mezzo-Staccato touch for the Right Hand inner part.
Write the Chord names above each bar.

THE MAMBO

The Mambo was a popular dance of the 1940's and 50's. It was the forerunner of the Cha-Cha-Cha but is now generally regarded as being too hard for the social dancer. It is therefore most often danced by Professional Ballroom dancers as an exhibition dance.

46. MAKE MINE MAMBO

CHORD TABLES

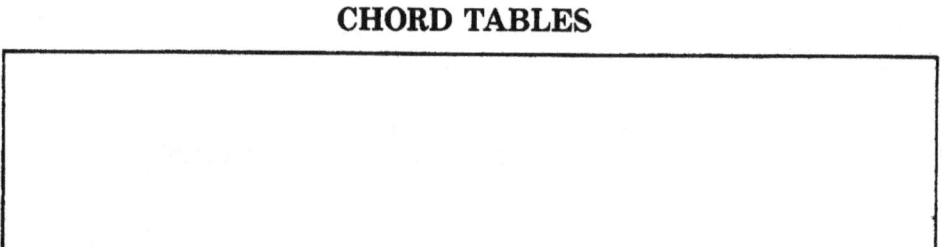

Write the Chord names above each bar.

POPULAR SHEET MUSIC

I'll Never Break Your Heart

The following piece is a contemporary 12/8 ballad performed by the vocal group **'Back Street Boys'**.

As it has been arranged for piano, the words are inserted between the two staves.

Harmonic Features

1) To achieve a rise in tension, the piece modulates to a key a semitone higher for the last chorus. This is a common device used by contemporary and jazz composers. The occurrence of these changes of key demonstrates the need for a good musician to have a knowledge of all keys and a wide range of chords. Popular music can be written in any key. The musician who wishes to play popular and jazz pieces must have as good a knowledge (if not better) of keys and chords as the musician who wishes to play the classics.

2) Also, note the use of the **I vi IV V** progression on the first page. Write the chord progression of the whole piece on manuscript to discover the reason for the pleasant sounds in this piece.

3) Also note the use of the minor (maj7) chord in bar 13. *Refer to the Contemporary Chord Workbook for information on this chord.*

Once you have learnt the written arrangement, use the chord pattern to:

1) experiment with the various rhythmic patterns given earlier in this book
2) build an improvised melody line of your own over the chord shapes.

Three Stave Sheet Music

Other sheet music you will come across will have 3 staves per line. One for the vocal line, and a Grand Staff for the piano part. If the accompaniment is different to the vocal line play it as written.

However if the vocal part is duplicated in the piano line there can be several approaches to the performance of the song:

1) Play the accompaniment part as written as a piano solo

2) Play the melody line (vocal line) as written, reading it from the upper third stave and improvise your own accompaniment based on the chord symbols. This version can be alternatively fuller or more sparse than the written version, depending on your ability to provide both the bass and chord elements of the accompaniment. You will also need to draw upon your knowledge of accompaniment styles and possibly a previous hearing of the song.

3) If accompanying a singer, it is recommended that you do not play the written melody line. Singers will feel more comfortable in the interpretation of the song if they are not restricted to the written note-values and exact pitches. Therefore, unless a singer specifically requests you play the melody line, which may happen at the practise stage, accompany the vocal line, with a fuller version of the bass and chord lines adding some decorative 'fills' where the melody is fairly static.

As I walked by you
Will you get to know me
A little more better?
Girl, that's the way love goes
And I know you're afraid
To let your feelings show
And I understand
But girl it's time to let go

I deserve a try, honey
Just one,
Give me a chance
And I'll prove this all wrong
You walked in
You were so quick to judge
But honey he's nothing like me
Darling why can't you see?

ADVANCED MODULATION SPIDER FOR A PIECE IN A MAJOR KEY

196

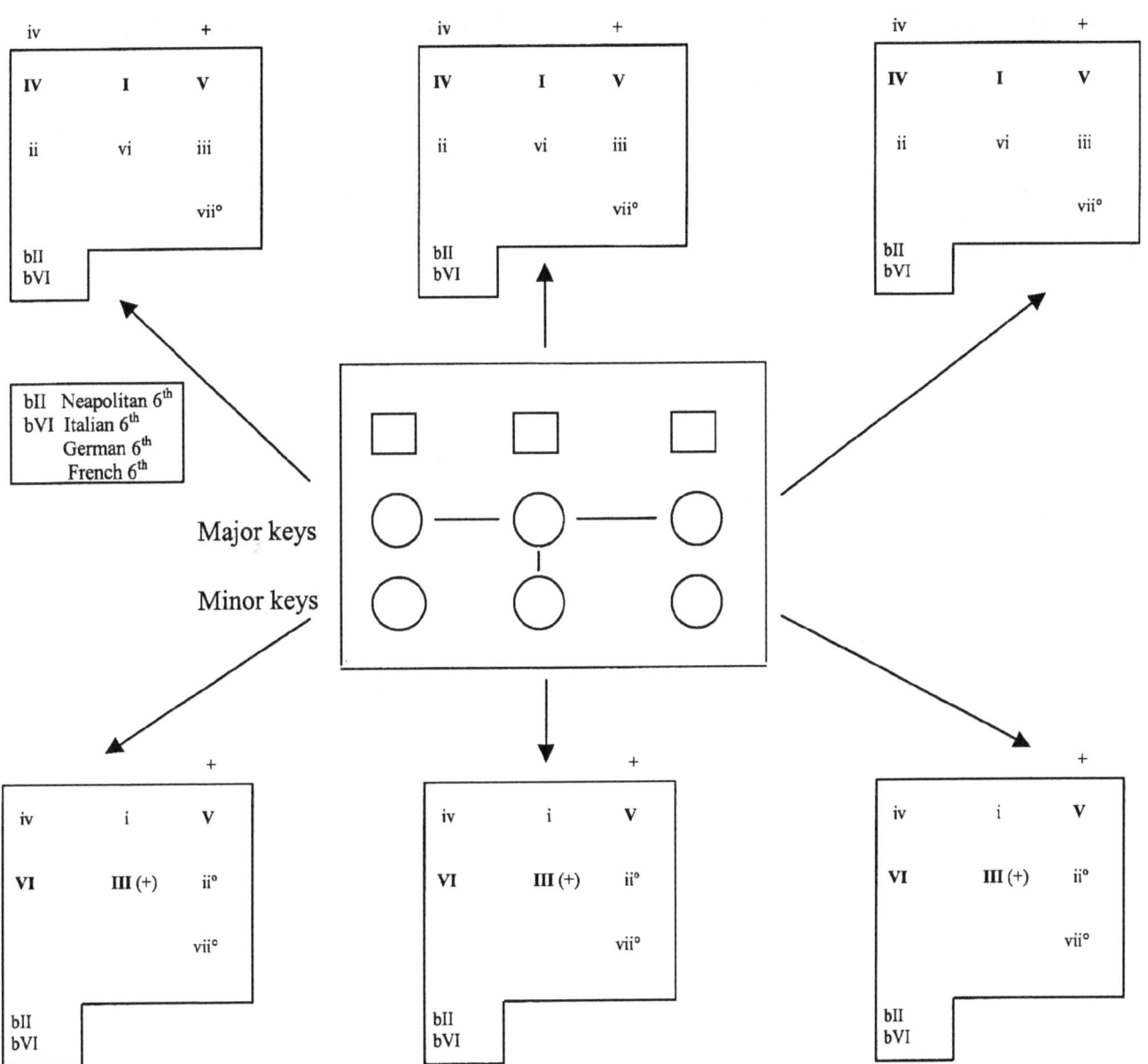

For information on, and pieces using chromatic chords (Neapolitan, Italian, German and French) refer to Book 3 of The Contemporary Piano Method by Margaret Brandman.

Colour Coding

When analysing any piece, you can colour code the keys by choosing one colour for each of the six keys. Add colour to each of the key centre circles.

Remember to place the *number* of sharps or flats for each key signature in the boxes.

Use this Modulation Spider Chart as a template. Owners of this book are permitted to photocopy this page for use with pieces in different keys.

© Copyright Dr. Margaret Brandman 2002

ADVANCED MODULATION SPIDER FOR A PIECE IN A MINOR KEY

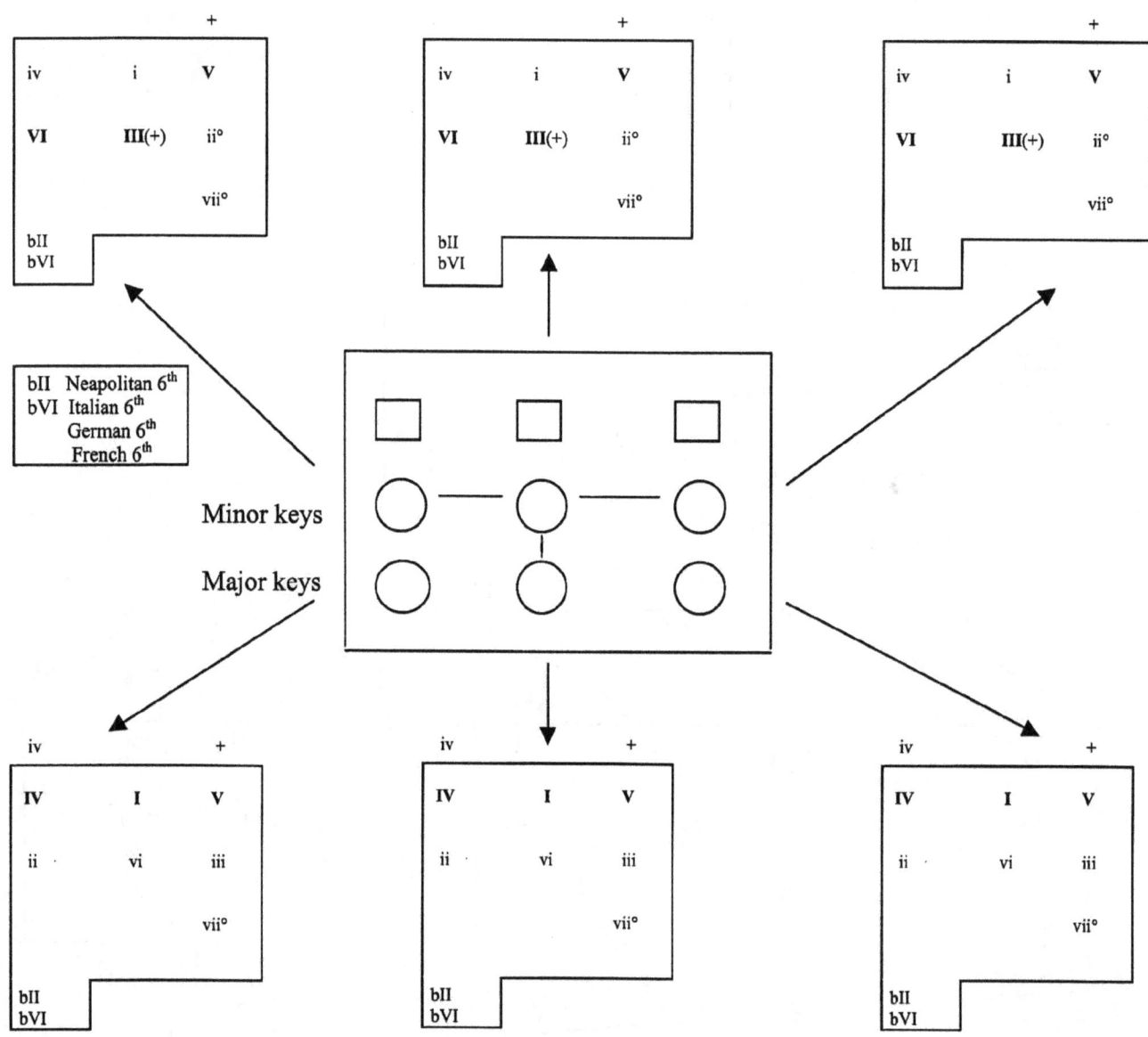

For information on, and pieces using chromatic chords (Neapolitan, Italian, German and French) refer to Book 3 of The Contemporary Piano Method by Margaret Brandman.

Use this Modulation Spider Chart as a template. Owners of this book are permitted to photocopy this page for use with pieces in different keys.

© Copyright Dr. Margaret Brandman 2002

SIGNS AND TERMS USED IN THIS VOLUME

STYLE MARKINGS

Con — with
Senza — without
Subito (Sub) — suddenly
Simile — continue in the same manner
Tacet — (Lat. silent) — do not play
poco a poco — little by little
Cantabile — in a singing style
Scherzando — playfully
Vivace — lively
Molto — much or very
Marcato — marked, stressed or accented
Legato — smoothly
Staccato — detached

SPEED INDICATIONS

Tempo — speed
Largo — very slowly
Lento — slowly
Adagio — leisurely
Andante — at an easy walking pace
Allegretto — moderately fast
Allegro — fast
Presto — very fast
Accelerando — gradually getting faster
Ritardando — gradually getting slower
Rallentando — gradually getting slower
Ritenuto — immediately slower
Moderato — moderately

SIGNS

1. Dynamics

Pianissimo (pp) — very soft
Piano (p) — soft
Mezzo Piano (mp) — moderately soft
Mezzo Forte (mf) — moderately loud
Forte (f) — loud
Fortissimo (ff) — loud

2. Touch

Mezzo-Staccato — half staccato
Staccato — detached
Staccatissimo — very short
Long heavy Accent — >
Short sharp Accent — ∧
Tenuto — held

3. Directions

Ottava (8va) — octave
8va Basso — an octave lower
Loco — in the usual place (play as written)
Da Capo (D.C.) — repeat from the beginning
Dal Segno (D.S.) — repeat from the sign
Al Fine — to the end
Al Coda — to Coda
M.M. — Maelzel's Metronome
INTRO — introduction

4. Ornaments   Refer to page:

Arpeggiando	48
Acciaccatura	54
Appogiatura	58
Trill	70
Mordent	79
Inverted Mordent	84
Tremolo	97
Turn	100
Inverted Turn	114
Glissando	139

SUGGESTED PRACTICE ROUTINE

By the time this book is completed, your daily practice schedule should include the following practical elements. Using a rotation plan similar to that given on the last page of Book 1 of the series, choose from 3 to 5 keys per day in which to practise all the elements.

SCALES

Similar Motion Scales

Major Scales — Compass: Two-Octaves
Natural, Harmonic and Melodic Minor Scales — Compass: One-Octave at first then extend to Two-Octaves.
The Blues Scale — Compass: One-Octave

Contrary Motion Scales

Major Scales — Compass: One-Octave at first then extend to Two-Octaves.
Harmonic Minor Scales — Compass: One Octave at first then extend to Two-Octaves.

Chromatic Scales

From any starting note. Compass: Two-Octaves.

CHORDS

1. **Triads** — Major, Minor, Diminished, Augmented and Suspended Fourth. Practise in Block and Broken forms as three-note and four-note chords, in all inversions.
2. **Sixths** — Major Sixth and Minor Sixth chords as four-note chords. Practise in all inversions in Block and Broken forms.
3. **Sevenths** — Dominant Seventh, Diminished Seventh, Major Seventh, Minor Seventh, Half-Diminished Seventh (Minor Seventh Flattened Fifth) and Dominant Seventh Suspended Fourth chords, in all inversions as four-note chords in Block and Broken forms.

See *Pictorial Patterns for Keyboard Scales and Chords* for a scale practice planner including all the scales and chords mentioned on this page.

Set up the planner for all keys.

MARGARET BRANDMAN'S

INTEGRATED SUPPORT MATERIALS FOR THIS LEVEL

TECHNICAL

* Pictorial Patterns for Keyboard Scales and Chords - *graphic patterns to help students learn the keyboard pathways for scales, along with helpful hints on fingering, and a specific practice planner for daily scale and chord practice.*

IMPROVISATION SKILLS

* Its Easy to Improvise - *information on how to add left hand accompaniments to single melody lines with chord symbols, and improvise or embellish a Right Hand line.*
Application to many gently graded well-known melodies and introducing many chord types. Providing more practice in the accompaniment skills employed on pages 42 and 43 of this book.

REPERTOIRE

• Dreamweaving - *each tuneful piece is composed with a varied set of technical challenges and features a different four note chord along with linked scales or modes.*

• Twelve Timely Pieces - *catchy performance pieces in varying time signatures from 2/4 to 7/4 and in major and minor key signatures up to two sharps and flats.*

• Contemporary Modal Pieces - *featuring unusual rhythms and interesting harmonies*

• Blues and Boogie-Woogie - *12 original blues and boogie pieces in major and minor keys, demonstrating various ways of writing the swing feel, and exploring many Left Hand boogie patterns.*

• Best of Hot Hits for Easy Piano - *easy arrangements of recent popular songs*

• Six Contemporary Pieces

• Reflections - *concert work for piano*

• Sonorities - *concert work for piano*

• Static Ripples - *Piano Duet*

THEORY/AURAL

• Contemporary Aural Course - Sets 2 to 6
• Contemporary Aural Course Set 7 - Hear Your Chords!
• Contemporary Aural Course Set 8 - Hear More Chords!
• Contemporary Theory Workbooks 1 and 2
• Contemporary Chord Workbook

Suggested Complementary Book on Rhythm: Modern Reading Text in 4/4 - Louis Bellson & Gil Breines

HANDY MANUSCRIPT PAGE

www.ingramcontent.com/pod-product-compliance
Lightning Source LLC
Chambersburg PA
CBHW081352160426
43198CB00015B/2587